FATHER, FORGIVE

FORGIVE

how to forgive the unforgivable

Robin Oake

Authentic

Reprinted 2008, 2010
First published 2007 by Authentic Media
Milton Keynes
www.authenticmedia.co.uk

British Library Cataloguing in Publication Data
A catalogue record for this book is available from the
British Library
ISBN 978-1-85078-765-5

Design by James Kessell for Scratch the Sky Ltd
(www.scratchthesky.com)
Printed in Great Britain by Cox and Wyman, Reading

In gratitude to God for and in memory of
Stephen
Special Branch Officer,
Greater Manchester Police,
who bravely laid down his life to save others

Dedicated to:
My daughter-in-law, Lesley and her children
Christopher, Rebecca and Corinne; Dorothy and
Neil; my daughters, Judi and Sue, and their
respective families
and to my dear wife, Chris

CONTENTS

PART 3: Forgiveness – How?

ACKNOWLEDGEMENTS

I am deeply grateful for the understanding and guidance of Mike Todd, Chief Constable of Greater Manchester Police, and his senior officers; the sympathetic help of Paul Kelly and his colleagues in the Police Federation, and the very many colleagues of Steve who expressed their sympathy and offered help through this trauma.

Of course, my deep gratitude to Revd Rob White and his wife, Marion, who have continued to look after Lesley and family and given counsel, sustenance, and been wonderfully good listeners. To my own pastor, Revd Jonathan Stanfield, and the leadership of our church for patience and counsel; to the congregations of Poynton, Hazel Grove, Altrincham and Hartfield churches in Cheshire and at Port St Mary in the Isle of Man, for their encouragement and prayer support.

Deep appreciation to Richard and Susan Williamson, and their musician friends who played so inspiringly as 'Wellspring' at the thanksgiving and funeral services.

For those who have encouraged me to write this short book and the many people who have had to listen to me speak, the notes for which have made up most of the content of its pages.

viii   *Acknowledgements*

To Sheila Jacobs who, as consultant editor, has been so patient, so innovative and inspiring and without whom, together with the belief of Charlotte Hubback (Authentic), this book would never have been seen.

Finally, I am so grateful to God for sustaining us as a family, giving strength and motivation to move on and enabling us to remember Steve with so many terrific memories. May his example be a continuing challenge and inspiration to us all.

FOREWORD

It was a dark January evening and my wife and I were watching the BBC News. A policeman, we heard, had been murdered in Manchester.

'Wonder if Steve knew him?' we asked one another.

We learned later from my brother-in-law, Robin Oake, that the victim was actually his son and our nephew, Stephen.

It is hard to describe the shock, confusion, the grief and the loss when something like this happens, but almost incredibly – and I think I speak for all members of our Christian family – there were no feelings of revenge or bitterness. Robin summed it up for us as well as for himself at the press conference next day when he said he had forgiven the person who had done this.

Many found this hard to believe, but it *is* true. In this book he tries to tell us in his own words how it can be true not just for us but for anyone who puts their trust in Christ. It's all down to the grace of God.

Forgiveness is so important for all those who hurt us as well as for those who have been hurt. At about the same time at Steve's death, I also saw a distraught woman on TV. She had lost her son to a murderous pae-dophile.

'I never can forgive him,' she said bitterly, and my heart went out to her.

'Poor woman,' I thought, 'she will destroy herself.' And, sadly, that could be the case.

Maybe, for one reason or another, that's where you find yourself – nursing some grudge or hurt or bitterness. If so, read on! The man who wrote this book did so from hard-won experience, with the prayer that what Christ has done for us as a family, he might do for you.

The Revd Dr J.F. Balchin
(formerly of Above Bar Church, Southampton,
Purley Baptist Church and London Bible College)

PART 1

My story

INTRODUCTION: The call

The insistent ringing of the phone gave no clue as to what I was about to hear.

Tuesday 14 January 2003. I was at home without any family. It was a cold dark evening, with a moaning gale outside. The telephone startled me for a moment; then when I picked up the receiver, I was surprised to hear Lesley, my daughter-in-law, speaking from Poynton.

'Robin, I've just been told by the police that Steve's been involved in an accident.'

'An accident?'

'I don't know any more detail. He's being taken to North Manchester Hospital. I'm just about to be picked up . . . I'll ring you later.'

I replaced the receiver in silence, wondering what had happened.

I had spoken on the phone with my policeman son, Steve, two days before. I'd been in Manchester visiting my youngest daughter, Sue, who was in hospital. He'd mentioned that he and his Special Branch colleagues had been warned that this Tuesday would be a difficult day. He had not spoken about anything specific – that was always a rule between us – but I knew, from what he said, it would be an early start.

Lesley and I assumed at first that Steve had had an accident in his car; I thought maybe he'd fallen asleep at the wheel. (Later, we discovered he had been up since 4 a.m. and, as was his daily practice, had had a quiet time of prayer and Bible reading before going on duty. In fact, he'd called into his local church to sing to his guitar rather than wake the house up!)

Chris, my wife, was in Altrincham looking after the grandchildren and Sue's husband, while she was recovering from surgery. So I was alone with my thoughts.

Nearly two hours later, the phone rang again.

This time, I heard sobbing.

'Lesley?'

'Robin, Steve's been murdered.'

My head spun. I blurted, 'What?' but after that, I couldn't speak.

Then Alan Green, later the Deputy Chief Constable of Greater Manchester Police, came on the phone.

'Robin, I'm so sorry to have to break the awful news like this.' He took a deep breath and told me the rest. Steve and his colleagues had been on a targeted operation. In making an arrest, he had been stabbed by one of the three suspects. Alan added that Steve had been extremely brave and probably saved the lives of his colleagues. He gave me the bare details of the tragedy. He was having difficulty in speaking; I sensed that he was in tears, just as I was.

I remember saying to him, 'Please, please look after Lesley.' And then, shocked, I could only pray.

1

Early days

I was born in Purley, Surrey, on 25 June 1937. Until I joined the Metropolitan Police, I lived in Hooley, a village five miles south of Purley, with my parents and two elder sisters, Cherry and Wendy, seven and two years older than me respectively. We had devoted parents who, even in austere times, provided well for us all.

My mother was a housewife. She had a trained contralto voice but was always too shy to use it except in a choir. My father was a senior executive in the then General Post Office. At seventeen, he'd won a competition to design a fully automatic telephone system; his winnings were just £5! I've often wondered, if only he had patented it, where would the family be now?

We saw little of Dad during World War Two, as he worked in the Underground Cabinet Office, dealing with communications for the Prime Minister, Mr Winston Churchill, and General Dwight D. Eisenhower. His hours were long and he slept in London most of the time, occasionally coming home for a day or two.

As a family, we were bombed out with a direct hit from a 'doodlebug' (flying bomb) which killed two of our neighbours and flattened three houses, severely damaging ours, in Church Lane Avenue. Dad was inside

at the time, home on two days' leave. Incredibly, he survived the ordeal, although he was injured. Afterwards,
we went to live with an aunt in Poole, Dorset. We
watched many of the preparations for D-Day in the harbour, as well as day-to-day operations of naval shipping,
and Sunderland Flying Boats in and out of the Channel.
Exciting times for a seven-year-old.

After the war, and back in our rebuilt house in Surrey,
my childhood took me to Chipstead Church to sing in
the choir and ring bells for the services. It was worth
7/6d (37½p) a Sunday. I also went to Sunday school but
was asked to leave after misbehaving. I believe the last
straw in my catalogue of bad behaviour was to tie a girl's
plaits to the back of a chair. This caused quite a rumpus
when she stood to sing!

At about the same time, my sister Cherry came home
from Nonington Physical Education College to tell the
family that she had become a Christian. None of us knew
how to respond to that. Although my parents sent us to
Sunday school as children, they were not church-goers at
that time; I think they thought they were Christian simply because they lived upright lives (although they were
both 'converted' later on). Still, the life-change in Cherry
was plain for all to see.

After my exclusion from Chipstead Sunday School, I
joined Crusaders in my teens. I tolerated the Sunday
afternoon Bible Class so I could participate in other
activities, including sport and camps. But it was while I
was a teenager at camp in Studland Bay, Dorset that I
became a Christian. Until then, I hadn't really noticed
and certainly not accepted the challenge to truly *follow*
Christ, even though my sister's evident life-change had
made me think.

I was in the camp with eight in a bell tent, and about
twelve tents in total. Each morning, there was a half-

hour session taken by a padre, a missionary who spoke on a particular theme . . . the cross of Jesus. Why the cross? Why Jesus on the cross? Sin and the cross; the cross in conversion and the cross in our daily life . . . or something very similar to that.

In the evening, there was a vibrant time of singing and testimonies. This was led by the commandant, Kenneth Anderson, with the padre taking the epilogue. It was here that I linked the life-change in the sister I respected so much with what the padre was saying. I knew then that I needed to actually *repent* of sin and ask Jesus to forgive and to be in my life. I saw that Jesus loved me and had died for my sin, so I went to the commandant and queried, 'Just *how* do I ask Jesus into my life?'

Soon after that, my other sister, Wendy, went to a mission in Redhill, heard evangelist Tom Rees, and became a Christian too.

I felt an immediate elation, but it gradually dawned on me more and more what a life-changing experience I had had. I think, for me, it wasn't so much 'I was blind but now I see' but 'It was very difficult to see but now I see much better!'

I knew I had to live up to 'being a Christian' but found it quite hard at school; there was no Christian Union. But Cherry organised a Bible study at home for young people which became a source of real strength and knowledge for me – nothing like this was organised by the local church. From that group, we met young people from Purley Baptist Church, where there was a lively minister and youth group leader, both of whom helped me and strengthened me in Christ before I joined the police service.

I'd passed the 11+ exam and attended Reigate Grammar School. But I left after GCEs to join the Civil Service in the Home Office (Prison Commission). That

gave me a taste of work in the field of justice; I even
thought about becoming a prison governor. But my sister Cherry started praying about my future, something I
confess I didn't think about doing at the time. With my
sister's encouragement, I did begin to pray regularly
about what I was to do with my life, and it wasn't long
before I was challenged to apply for the Metropolitan
Police. I joined them on 24 June 1957. Interestingly, I had
been declared 'medically unfit' for National Service
(although the War Office would not disclose why and an
appointment in Harley Street could find nothing physi-
cally wrong with me) but the Police Medical Board
found me fully fit and passed me at the interview. To me,
that was confirmation of being in the right place.

By this time, I'd met my future wife, Chris, through
Purley Baptist Church. Chris had become a Christian as
a teenager as a result of the testimony of Helen
Roseveare, a Congo missionary. Before I joined the
police, Chris had started her nursing training at St
Thomas's Hospital in London – she eventually became a
matron. Anyway, this meant with our shifts, we courted
at some very peculiar hours. We married on 1 April 1961,
by which time I was working in Scotland Yard. Stephen
was born on 21 April 1962, Judi on 14 August 1963 and
Sue on 1 May 1965.

I stayed with the Metropolitan Police until I was a
chief inspector, having also been a sergeant in the notorious 'C' Division (Soho and Mayfair), then an instructor
at the Training School, having also worked in Brixton
Division. I was very fortunate to have had three years in
the rank of Inspector at University College, London
reading law on a scholarship awarded at Bramshill
Police Staff College.

As a family we attended Purley Baptist Church where
first Judi became a Christian and then Steve too started

following Christ. Sue became a Christian sometime later, when we'd moved to Manchester.

Steve had been coming to church regularly but I knew that he wasn't all that keen. There were some Sundays when he would look for any excuse not to come with us. I didn't blame him; if it hadn't been that I got paid for singing in the choir and bell-ringing, I doubt that I would have been so keen to go to church when I was his age.

However, when Steve was fifteen, he watched the film *A Thief in the Night* (a good title for a budding police officer!). He told us afterwards that it struck him that he didn't really *know* Jesus Christ as his parents and some of his contemporaries did. He had never known anything about his wrongdoing, what the Bible calls 'sin', being forgiven. Churchgoing was a formality without any relationship with God, although I know he did enjoy the youth activities through the week and some weekends. Anyway, Steve came to the point where he realised that being brought up in a Christian family didn't mean he automatically had a friendship with God and a ticket to heaven. He knew he needed to say sorry to God and get right with him, and when he did, he 'came alive in Christ'. After that, churchgoing was no longer a boring ritual but a delight, as he worshipped with fellow believers. That start in his Christian life enabled him to enjoy daily Bible reading and private prayer and later to seek God's purpose in life for him.

Little did we know then what that purpose would include.

2

Happy family

In the police service, there are often moves between different Force areas. Having been away from London Metropolitan in Hampshire on the Directing Staff at the National Police College, I was commended to apply for a post as superintendent in Greater Manchester Police. Here I was to joint-head a new department in a proposed and novel Community Contact Section, probably one of the first in the UK. Consequently, I transferred north in July 1978, with the family to follow. Steve had been working hard with odd jobs to save enough money for a trip to Texas in the United States; so I felt really sorry for him that on his return he came up to Manchester without being able to share his five-week American experience with his old friends from church and school.

The establishment of the new department was to take a year; but once we were up and running, with fourteen satellite local departments in the Divisions working well, Derrick Johnson – my fellow superintendent – and I were dispersed elsewhere, he to Bury and I to Moss Side. My predecessor had been shot at while in his office. When I entered his old room in Moss Side Police Station (later renamed as Greenheys) I was rather stunned to see the bullet-hole still in the glass.

We bought a house in Timperley, Cheshire. Steve immediately started at the Sixth Form College at Wellington Road School, Judi at Altrincham Grammar School and Sue at Delahays. We had heard of the lively fellowship at Altrincham Baptist Church and began to go there.

Two years later, Steve left school. He had already met Lesley Thompson, who had also been at Wellington and was now working with NatWest Bank. She was also Miss Altrincham in the year they started courting – what a catch!

Steve's first working experience was with a cartography firm in Sale but through some lost contracts, he and two others were made redundant. He then began work in an electrical retail shop in Altrincham, but he told us that he felt he needed a bigger challenge, even though he enjoyed his work very much. Meanwhile, he'd got engaged to Lesley, and they were married on 23 April 1983 – two days after his twenty-first birthday. They bought a small terraced house in Macclesfield, Cheshire, a good first step on the property ladder, and later moved to their home in Poynton, about ten miles south-east of the City of Manchester. My wife and I grew very fond of Lesley; a clever lady, she became a terrific daughter-in-law and then the mother of three.

One day in 1984, I was in my office at Police Headquarters in Manchester when a fellow Assistant Chief Constable, Paul Whitehouse (later, Chief Constable of Sussex) wandered in at lunchtime and said, 'Had a good interview with your son this morning, Robin.'

I was surprised. 'Oh, yes? What's he been up to?'

Paul smiled. 'Didn't you know? He applied for the police and he has been accepted – excellent quality.'

Wow, that was real news to me. That evening I telephoned Steve at his home and congratulated him on his appointment.

'Why didn't you tell me that you were applying?' I asked.

'Dad,' he said, 'I didn't want it *ever* thought that you had had an influence on my appointment. Lesley and I had prayed this through and if this was right for us, then we knew I'd be accepted.'

So Steve went to Bruche Police Training School near Warrington in 1984. And when he was on that final parade having passed his exams and done so well in his practical training, I was a very proud dad.

As an Assistant Chief Constable, I had many public meetings either to attend or address. On one particular evening, I was in Moss Side where, some time before, I had been the superintendent. Following the meeting, I dropped into the old station at Greenheys. As I drank tea with my former colleagues in the front office in walked Steve with a sergeant. It was a magic moment as it was the first time I had met Steve on duty.

There was a stunned silence as we looked at each other. It probably only lasted for a moment but to me it seemed much longer.

Then the sergeant broke the silence.

'Go on, Steve. Put a good word in for me!'

Some time later, I was driving home from a late night at Police Headquarters – about 11.30 p.m. – and, in Barlow Moor Road, Chorlton-cum-Hardy, I saw a small crowd outside a public house with a police van nearby. There was a fight, and a police officer in uniform was standing alone in the centre of the melee. I slammed on my brakes and ran back to see if I could assist. As I was nearing the crowd I saw it was Steve, head and shoulders above the rest. Then it clicked.

'He can't be alone,' I said to myself, 'police van, Steve's not a police driver yet . . . there *must* be a colleague there.

If I wade in, he'll never live it down that Dad came to the rescue!'

He didn't see me as I slunk back to my car.

I never did tell him about the incident though he told me one day about that fight: 'It was nothing,' he said, nonchalantly. 'We sorted it out.'

Soon after that, Steve told me about something else that happened. He was the front-seat passenger in a police van when a middle-aged woman waved it down and yelled that there was headless man lying in the gutter round the corner.

Steve got out (I think with some trepidation) and went with the woman to the corner of the road. She pointed out the corpse. Cautiously, Steve approached. He could see that she was right – the fully clothed man had no head! With a lump in his throat and remembering that a Training School sergeant had told his class they should 'expect the unexpected', he closed in, thinking about what to do with a death in the street . . . Then he relaxed. The man wasn't headless; he wasn't even dead. He was looking inside a drain for his lost car keys. What a relief!

Steve eventually joined the Traffic Department. That meant a much wider patrol, including the motorways. He was not averse to popping in to see his sisters, sometimes on duty, for a cup of tea. Of course the children loved to see Uncle Steve in uniform especially if he 'accidentally' switched on the blues and twos.

At church, he and Lesley were very much involved in leading worship. Lesley, very accomplished and confident, encouraged Steve who wouldn't have naturally been 'up front'. He had learnt to play the trumpet and French horn at school, and used those skills often with the music group. He was in a local band, too, sitting alongside his son Christopher in the trumpet section.

As a family, we have always been very close. Fortunately, Lesley's side of the family all lived within a short driving distance and, until 1986, so did my daughters and my wife and I. We all got on well, even after we moved to the Isle of Man, when we were a flight or a sea-ferry journey away. I have so many happy family memories of Steve; for instance, one day, Christopher, Steve and I were playing golf together. This only happened very infrequently since we'd moved to the island. Christopher was about thirteen and on this memorable day we had had a fairly even match. But at the eighteenth hole at Davenport, Christopher hit his second shot to within two feet of the flag and holed the putt for a birdie. This meant that he had beaten his dad and me on the same day. I can still hear his whoops of delight.

What part did forgiveness play in my life back then? Well, I was not the world's best husband, dad, father-in-law, granddad or uncle. I have had to be forgiven much through my family life and, indeed, in my job and other interests that I have had. I've made mistakes, done things which have hurt others . . . I don't deserve forgiveness yet within the family and from God, I have known the very real release that forgiveness brings. In my marriage, my wife and I have always been clear about any tension that we have – it can't last longer than a few hours because we regularly pray together.

So, then as now, forgiveness was a part of my life as a practising Christian, not a 'big deal' at all. But the big test was to come, and come it did, that terrible night when our beloved Steve was killed in the line of duty.

3

Tragedy

The January night was dark and blank. I was numb.

I had to take in the shocking news of Steve's death, and it was proving impossible. Hurt, devastated . . . it was unbelievable. Then I came to and realised that it was not long before the 10 o'clock News on TV. I had to tell Chris before she saw it on the screen.

I had always insisted that my police officers should never give bad news by telephone but this had to be an exception. I hesitated – I had to think of what to say. How *do* you say something like that? But I knew I had to let my wife hear it from me. I was in tears and finding breathing difficult as I phoned Sue's house. Dave, her husband, answered. I could tell by his voice that he didn't yet know the news so I asked to speak to Chris.

'Darling, I have some dreadful news. Please be strong as you always are.' And then I told her: 'Our Steve has been murdered on duty.'

It seemed her breath had gone. I sensed from her breathing that she was heartbroken. She was stunned; of *course* she was – but she very bravely asked, 'How?'

I stammered out what I knew. We had a long silence and then prayed together.

How do you deal with such devastation? I simply said, 'The Lord is with you, but I must ring Judi. Will you somehow get a message to Sue or stop her seeing the News tonight? And be careful when you tell dear Natalie and Joshua; they'll miss Steve *so* much . . . It might be an idea to get to Poynton to see Lesley . . . and the kids.'

Then I had to tell Judi at Gorstage. Poor thing. She just burst into tears and uncontrollable sobs. But she, too, very bravely asked how it happened and incredibly, thinking of others, asked if anyone else was hurt. She knew how much this news would affect Matthew, her husband, and their two daughters, Sophie and Olivia who so loved their Uncle Steve.

I felt empty, alone and ill but, yes, I knew God was with me. I kept telling myself this. I phoned Jonathan Stanfield, my pastor at Port St Mary Baptist Church, and my prayer partner, Malachy Cornwell-Kelly. I also phoned my good friends Will and Hilary Costain and they, plus Ken Quane, arrived very quickly.

We watched the 10 o'clock News. It was sombre but it seemed so matter-of-fact to say that a 'Special Branch officer in Manchester had been killed during a terrorist raid and a number of his colleagues were injured.' My friends and I talked for a while and then we knelt in prayer in the lounge.

Some time later, the front doorbell rang and I opened up to Neil Kinrade, my former colleague in the Island Force, the then Deputy Chief Constable, and a good friend. He was at his home but had been told the news officially from our Police Headquarters and was requested to come to Ballakillowey to give me the information. He had no idea that I already knew. Neither did he know that Chris was away, so he'd brought Inspector Carolyn Kinrade to be with her. They came into the lounge and joined us in prayer where, amongst other things, we were praying especially for Lesley and the children, Christopher, Becki and Cozzie. We were also praying for Chris, Judi and Sue and their families and Steve's Special Branch colleagues who been seriously injured.

We prayed too for the alleged killer, though at that stage we had no information as to who he was or where he came from. Much later, after Neil and Carolyn had left with my other friends, except for Jonathan and Ken, we sat and talked and prayed again for Lesley and the children and for Chris, Judi and Sue. We also prayed hard for Lesley's mum and stepfather. That night, although I tried to sleep, but my head was pounding, asking unanswerable questions, trying to imagine the scene where Steve had been – any sleep was impossible.

I tossed and turned and eventually got up and prayed and read parts of the Bible, hardly seeing what I had in front of me. I recalled Steve's words about a difficult day and later learnt from Lesley that the operation to which he'd referred had been successful. Then, having returned to his office, he and others in Special Branch were asked to attend a briefing in the afternoon for another raid in the evening. Steve had told Lesley that he would therefore be back much later than expected but he gave no details of extra duty.

Here at home, feeling empty, I was tearfully facing breakfast with Jonathan and Ken. I kept trying to piece together what might have happened and wondering how it could have been avoided. I tried to picture Steve with his colleagues, struggling to subdue a fighting-mad prisoner with a knife who was attempting to escape . . . my mind couldn't take it all in except that I had to simply bow my head and say in prayer, 'Lord, I don't know who he is but give me the grace to forgive the man who killed Steve.' I had no idea then that this would soon become public knowledge.

At 7.15 a.m., I had a call from Neil Kinrade to say that the media had chartered two planes and were coming en bloc to the Island. Would I be prepared to meet them? I naturally hesitated but listened to Neil's counsel that a press conference would satisfy the press, radio and TV in one session; difficult though it would be, it would be a great step forward to be able to talk about it. So I agreed, without enthusiasm. Consequently, a press conference was arranged at Port Erin Police Station for 9.30 a.m. Jonathan came with me.

I'd typed out a two-page statement for the media to read before I spoke, outlining what I had heard from Manchester and how the news was broken to me. I felt that the more the reporters knew before I faced them, the better.

The room was strangely quiet as we entered and Neil Kinrade opened the conference, expressing the deep sympathy of the Isle of Man Constabulary to our family. He talked briefly about what he had learnt from Manchester and then I thanked the press for coming and for being so evidently sensitive. Then the questions began. Mostly these were showing concern for Lesley and the family, asking about my wife and where she was and also about Judi and Sue. It was all very subdued and quite unlike any other press conference I'd been involved in during my police service.

Then one TV reporter simply asked, 'Mr Oake, what do you think about the man who killed your son?'

I took some time, I remember, to put words together; I had anticipated a question like that, so it wasn't as if I was unprepared. But I was still unsure as to exactly what I would say. I wanted to sound strong and sincere. I think I said something like, 'I don't know the man or all the circumstances of the operation but from my heart I forgive him.'

I heard another journalist say, 'You what?'

So I repeated what I had said. I wanted everyone in the room to hear it plainly: 'I forgive him.' I added, 'I'll be praying that God will forgive him too.'

'But he's a terrorist!'

'Don't you realise what he's done to you and your family?'

'Why do you forgive him?'

These new questions were not in any way rude or intrusive but they hurt and probably caused me to waver. I was not far from breaking down completely and tears were overflowing no matter how hard I blinked.

And yet, inside, I knew what I was saying was true. Yes, from long experience I knew the truth: Revenge imprisons us; forgiveness sets us free.

I came to that Conference with a deep-seated peace in my heart and mind. I had no acrimony even though I knew how much Lesley and the family, Chris and my daughters would be hurting. I sensed that many of our friends and, of course, Steve's colleagues, especially those who worked with him, would be grieving. But in the midst of all this, although I *felt* very weak, in an incredible way, I experienced a strength which could have only come from God.

4

'Where were you, God?'

When the journalists left the station, I gave an interview to Manx Radio which I believe was televised for Border TV. Again, I was pressed about forgiveness.

The local press representatives were well known to me and I counted them as friends; I think they knew me well enough not to be *too* surprised that as a Christian I would say what I did. Word spread also to two journalists from the *Daily Mail* who had missed the press conference but had come to my house. They asked about forgiveness and were persistent in further questions about my faith – about my church, about being a Christian in the police force. I found they were respectful and they did not overstay their welcome.

Back home, I rang Chris and found that Judi had come to be with her. I was sad not to be able to speak to the very sick Sue. I thought, sadly, that this news would not aid her recovery one bit. Chris had been to see Lesley and spent time with the children. Lesley's mother had also gone to the Poynton home. I longed to be with them all.

That afternoon, I flew to Manchester with Carolyn Kinrade who had, very generously, been given leave to spend time with Chris and the family. Our pastor,

Jonathan, and also a good friend, Joan Quane, came over too and spent the day with us; Jonathan and I had a very special time, walking together in Dunham Park, talking, praying, reminding ourselves of the promises of God and recognising that he never leaves us.

The next day we all had a dreadful time visiting the place where Steve had died and to say 'goodbye' in the hospital mortuary. It was almost too painful but the assurance was in our hearts that Steve had his reward in heaven; for he had known the Lord Jesus personally and had walked with him for many years, and so we took comfort from the promise of Jesus: 'He that believes in me will live, even though he dies' (Jn. 11:25).

On the Sunday, just five days later, at Poynton Baptist Church, hundreds crammed in to hear Pastor Rob White conduct a wonderfully uplifting service. The 'Wellspring' musicians sensitively led the songs, along with the group Steve had played his trumpet with. The service was not just to remember Steve and the family, but to be *positive* about what had happened.

Rob asked several questions which might have been on our lips, under the banner headline, 'OK God, what were you up to?' then, 'Why the good 'uns and the young 'uns?' and 'So, is it worth living for you?' But the one which really struck home was: 'Where were you, God, when Steve died last Tuesday?'

'God has assured us,' said Rob 'that he'll never let us down. He'll never walk off and leave us.'

God hadn't left Steve that night; Steve was there and God was there.

It was a moving time, with many of Steve's Special Branch colleagues who had specially come to our son's home church, and many others who knew the family. The media were also there but they were not intrusive in any way with microphones or cameras. Lesley came to the platform and added a brave postscript, talking about Steve and their very happy marriage. And she said, 'I want you all to know that God is just as real to me today as he was last week. He doesn't change.'

Next day, it was meant to be a short memorial service in the Special Branch offices at Manchester Airport. But word had got round and there were so many staff who knew Steve – from cleaners, catering folk and ground-staff, to pilots, air-hostesses and security personnel – that the service was moved to the extensive Airport Chapel. When we arrived, it was packed with about eight rows of people standing round the walls.

The chaplain, with much feeling and understanding, having known Steve well, involved police in reading the Bible and paying tribute to our son. It was so moving to hear of some who had found faith in Jesus through Steve's testimony; how young Christians had been helped by his witness and counsel; how others knew of Steve's Christian commitment by his attitude, his listening ear and his humour. We, as a family, were very moved.

Chief Constable, Mike Todd had recommended that Manchester Cathedral be used for the funeral and the Dean was very helpful with the arrangements. Lesley was clear about the order and content, even to the suggestion of Wintley Phipps coming from Florida to sing *No Need to Fear*. My good friend Graham Ferguson Lacey – who had been instrumental in the release of the hostage Terry Waite – paid Wintley's fare and also chartered a plane from the Isle of Man which carried the President, Chief Minister and many others from the Island.

As the cortege arrived at the cathedral, with six grey horses from the Greater Manchester Police at the front, we could hear the lively music being relayed to the hundreds of people outside the cathedral. It was so daunting yet there was a spring in my step because I knew it was to be a service of Christian witness to police colleagues and to a much wider audience.

With Rob White conducting the service, Paul Beasley-Murray and Roger Martin participating, former pastors at Altrincham and Poynton respectively and 'Wellspring' providing the wonderful music, the funeral was a great celebration of Steve's life. Prime Minister Tony Blair and his wife Cherie were there – Steve had been part of his protection team at one time – which was a great privilege. Mr Blair has been a constant encouragement in the years following Steve's death and we have been most grateful for that.

Our wider family was together and it was incredible that Sue, unwell though she was, was able to come to the cathedral. There was a sense of moving on, of forgiveness, of rejoicing through grief. Then the new Bishop of Manchester, the Rt Revd Nigel McCullock, whose very first service this was, pronounced the benediction.

Had we gone to that funeral still bursting with anger and resentment, it would have been a distressing time for everyone and a very mournful, miserable service. We would have regretted that for the rest of our lives. A thousand-strong congregation watching a grieving family seething with anger, seeking retribution, demanding answers – how would that have shown the love and forgiveness of Christ, and the hope we have for eternal life?

We wanted the world to know that Steve died simply doing his duty, so bravely, and that duty was part of his Christian life. Of *course* there was sadness for us all, but nevertheless this celebratory funeral was to evidence triumph through tragedy. Steve could well have said, with the apostle Paul, 'For to me, to live is Christ and to die is gain' (Phil. 1:21). And, as the congregation was welcomed, it was underlined that for Christians, death is never 'goodbye' but 'see you later'.

5

The journey

Almost two years afterwards, we attended the trial of the man who was subsequently found guilty of killing Steve. It was an arduous three and a half months at the Old Bailey. To sit within a few feet of the man in the dock was an eerie ordeal but it made me all the more determined to pray for him.

The full circumstances of the planned operation and subsequent arrest in Crumpsall, which was linked with a raid in north London, were meticulously outlined by the prosecution but the evidence was strenuously denied by Defence counsel.

The man was found guilty by a unanimous jury verdict and the subsequent terrorism trial involving him and others and a following unsuccessful appeal meant that the public was ignorant of the details for nearly three years.

The Michael Winner Trust arranged for a memorial to be sited outside the building where Steve was killed, which was a very generous gesture and very much appreciated. Though it was three and a half years after the incident, it was still a very daunting occasion to revisit Crumpsall. The ceremony was dignified but again brought back terrible memories. While there is some

measure of gratitude that Steve bravely gave his life for
his colleagues that awful day, to see his name on a
memorial stone filled my eyes with tears yet again.

Within six months, the stone had been desecrated and
smashed and its marble pieces thrown at police vehicles.
It was another bitter pill to swallow but, as always with
anything regarding our Steve, it presented further open-
ings, when people showed their sympathy, to speak
about God's grace – his free, unearned favour and love
for us, and his goodness.

To this day, my commitment is to pray for the man
who was found guilty of killing our son. The deep
wound of losing Steve in the prime of his life has left its
scars on all the close and wider family and, of course, on
his colleagues who were also very brave that day, and
badly injured. The healing process is long but we say
with confidence that we are being renewed by the powerful love and strength of the God who promised he
would always be with us.

In forgiving Steve's killer, I cannot say it was an easy
decision; forgiveness isn't natural when such a desperate
tragedy happens within a family. Just imagine how it
was for Lesley – to lose her husband of twenty years; for
the three teenage children to suddenly have their dad
taken from them; for Lesley's parents, Neil and Dorothy,
to lose their son-in-law; for Judi and Sue to lose the
brother they grew up with; for parents to lose their firstborn and only son. All of us have such wonderful memories; all of us know this unhealable wrench. Yet I have
learnt that bitterness, hatred, revenge and a never-to-be-
forgiven attitude are not the answer. You just *cannot*
move forward with such attitudes.

Even as we returned to the scene of the crime for the
unveiling of the memorial to Steve, I had to ask myself
the question again, 'Have I really and honestly forgiven

the killer?' I thought about it long and hard but even through the returning tears, I said in my heart and mouthed the words, 'Yes, Lord, I have forgiven him.' And, again, the vandals who mutilated the memorial stone and chucked the bits at police cars, breaking their windows . . . Whoever it was, and despite the renewed pain, I have to say that if I can forgive a murderer, I can certainly forgive mindless vandals. Yet I believe my forgiveness shouldn't preclude the police and the courts from meting out just punishment if the offenders are found. (One memorial that is hidden from the public eye is within the Police Training School at Sedgley Park where a wing has been named after Stephen. The plaque there reminds those who read it of his very happy life as father, brother, son and uncle, and of his daily Christian commitment.)

We, I suppose, would naturally ask God, 'Why?' *Why* did this have to happen? But I doubt we would know the answer this side of heaven. Much more to the point is the question, 'What now, Lord?' and 'Now that this has happened, how can we best live for you?' In other words, *how* can we move on?

As a police officer, I was always intrigued by the number of incidents which were fairly innocuous but escalated way out of proportion, usually because the parties involved stood on their rights, blamed others and no one would back down, even when a simple 'sorry' or 'let's sort it out' would very often have meant the heat being taken out of an argument. I doubt, however, that many other instances would have been in that category. The serious assaults and even murder or manslaughter, death by dangerous driving, arson and the one hundred and one other matters which make up an officer's daily life could not have been rectified by a simple apology. In my experience, it would rarely have entered my head in such situations to seek any appeasement while making enquiries, seeking evidence or preparing papers for court hearings.

The number of bombing incidents in central London where I worked for years and the isolated but serious terrorist incidents in later years, where you could only think of the group behind the bombings, rather than an individual, have meant that in these traumas I had never considered the implications of forgiveness. Yes, forgiveness had been part of family life, but then, we had never experienced the devastation of someone in the family being unlawfully killed; we knew nothing of the pain, that special kind of grief and the deep, deep heartache that such a death brings. It is the sort of trauma that, I suppose, we knew could happen to anyone, especially if some of us were police officers or in any other confrontational occupation. But while it was always a possibility it was never expected . . . until that dreadful day when our son was murdered while on duty.

With the numbness, the emptiness and the tears that this brought to our family, it started a new exploration in my mind which began to evolve within a couple of hours of the news of Steve's death reaching me. I immediately thought of the person who stabbed him though I had no picture in my head as to what he was like or who he was; I knew that many friends and former colleagues would be wondering how this would affect us but the word that constantly whispered itself in my head was 'forgiveness' and the search in my heart has continued ever since.

I have written this book to invite you to join me on the journey. From the outset, I have to tell you that I believe the word 'forgiveness' is largely a forgotten and certainly a neglected word – the forgotten F word, in fact. I want you, the reader, to share and try to understand the pain, but I hope to also quietly show you that when we suffer so greatly, the only way forward for any of us is, I believe, complete and unconditional forgiveness. This can bring healing of mind and even body.

So come with me as we explore the 'why' and learn the 'how' of forgiveness. Why should we, and how can we? Be prepared to be challenged – and encouraged.

PART 2

Forgiveness – Why?

INTRODUCTION:
The forgotten F word

We live in a world where, strangely, it is far easier to be confrontational, argumentative and unforgiving than to live at peace with one another. We see this within the family, in our villages and towns, at work, in leisure, on TV and in the newspapers, at national and international levels. We could get a clue about the nature of the world from the fact that so many are employed in a variety of organisations answering complaints – and from the number of lawyers who make a living out of litigation which, in many instances, is a first instead of a last resort.

In many of the fictional dramas on stage or at the cinema (and perhaps more especially in the 'soaps' and other entertainment on TV, which are meant to depict the society and the real situations of today), it is a deliberate ploy by the writers to increase the tension by retaliation, revenge, open wounds of non-forgiveness and actual or implied threats. 'I'll *never* forgive him!' Dramatic enough in dialogue, and probably designed to hook the viewer in so they don't miss the next episode, but when it mirrors everyday life it's not exciting – it's tragic. Yes, it is natural to disagree in certain circumstances; we cannot always be right. Yet sometimes, to disagree appeals to our basic nature which insists that 'I am right and you are wrong'.

As a police officer, certainly in my early days on the beat, I was frequently called to homes perhaps more than anywhere else to sort out what seemed to me to be a minor matter which should never have ended in tears. I was often exchanging names and addresses and referring the 'injured' party to the Magistrates' Court for the Justices to settle disputes. Occasionally, I was able to weigh up both arguments and suggest, at the very least, that a compromise could be reached. However, it was *very* rare for someone to back down and say 'I'm sorry.'

Later in my career, as Assistant Chief Constable, and then, more especially, in the top job, I was called to preside in disciplinary hearings. It was common for a constable or sergeant to appear in front of me who, had they simply backed down in a dispute and apologised, could have had the matter settled immediately; but no, they would take an unbending stand until the bitter end. Matters soon get out of hand where there is no remorse or where threat of retaliation is on the tip of the tongue.

Before Steve was killed, both the area and the principle of forgiveness had intrigued me. I often wondered if I were caught up in a serious situation – if my wife or any member of the family were unjustly hurt or wrongly accused – whether I could always forgive. Would I, like the soaps, want retribution? How would *I* feel, in reality, when confronted with the emotions of anger, criticism, hatred and the big question, 'Why?'

Why forgive?

In this section, let me help you see that there is a way of release of tension from past hurts and present problems, a way out of the cycle of violence and despair that comes from not being able to let go, through taking the admittedly difficult step of forgiveness . . . either in the offering of it, or in the receiving of it.

1

Forgive and forget?

I have been asked on several occasions during my police career why, as a Christian, I haven't forgiven offenders instead of reporting or arresting them for an offence they have committed. The answer, to my mind, is very clear – the law is in place to protect the innocent. And as one who was employed to uphold the law on behalf of the government and law-abiding citizens of the country, it was not within my remit – or that of any police officer of whatever rank – to forgive.

Justice must be done

There is certainly opportunity at times for leniency or mitigation regarding issuing a caution, a verbal warning or even taking no further action, and such decisions are within the legal framework. However, where there has been a breach of the law, forgiveness or complete exoneration is not within the compass of police whose privileged position is to see that justice is done.

A law-breaker offends the standards set by central or local government. Both criminal and civil law have evolved through centuries to suit the day and place where they govern so that people know the boundaries within which they can reasonably live. They can also know the boundaries which should limit others – those who seek to intrude on another's privacy, are greedy, or those who wish to assault others or to indulge in their lusts. Law describes guidelines and while it has been argued that 'ignorance of the law is no defence', most law is, after all, common sense and reasonable people should know where they stand.

Even the Courts have no power to forgive, although they have more room to manoeuvre than a police officer; much statute law offers a range of penalties – a minimum and a maximum – so that magistrates and judges have a considerable leeway when sentencing a person found guilty of an offence or, in civil litigation, determining suitable compensation from those who have been found to be unreasonable or unscrupulous.

So, the essential point I am driving at is: letting the culprit completely 'off the hook' is not within the law's remit.

As a sergeant in the West End of London, I had a constable working for me who was an active Christian. His testimony was clear in the station and in the Christian Police Association though, sadly, he was a little diffident about his decision-making. I thought that with experience he could have a bright career ahead of him.

However, while I was patrolling in the Soho area I had a call on my radio to return to the station to meet an inspector. He told me in no uncertain terms that this constable was not worth the uniform he was wearing. Why? He had seen a beggar in Oxford Street sitting on the pavement in ragged clothing, offering a plastic cup to passers-by, pleading for money. This was in the days of the Vagrancy Act 1824 which contained a section which was unusual in that it said, among other things, that 'a

constable not only may but MUST arrest any person begging in a street or public place.' The constable had witnessed the begging and, feeling sorry for the man, had
put money in his cup, not arrested him or even moved
him on – a direct contravention of the Act.

A shopper had watched this extraordinary action by
the officer and complained to the police station, quoting
the number on the officer's shoulder. So, here I was with
an irate inspector, who was not enamoured with
Christians anyway, ordering me to deal with this evident
disciplinary offence. Not easy; I knew that the officer
was in some way trying to be compassionate. But I also
knew he should not try to reconcile his beliefs with this
particular police duty. I did speak with him at length and
he recognised that he was finding it very difficult. He
said he felt sorry for too many unfortunates and found it
was impossible for him to 'walk by on the other side'. It
was not surprising, therefore, that he resigned soon after.
Following college training he was ordained and, later,
became an Army chaplain.

Duty and compassion

Police have a duty to perform. Try to imagine the chaos
there would be if police began to forgive law-beakers,
just letting them go! It would soon lead to all sorts of corruption, favouritism, bribery and turning a blind eye.
Where would it end? Having said that, I have experienced a real emotion of sympathy at many crime scenes;
I know in other circumstances I would have cried with
the offender.

The early hours of Christmas Day seemed for many
years to be an invitation to call the superintendent out of
bed. So I wasn't surprised, on one of those frosty, cold

and dark mornings at 4.40 a.m. to be woken by the shrill ringing of the phone. I was being called out to an address near Alexandra Park, Moss Side.

'Sir, suspicious death. Before you enter the house, you ought to know it's not a pleasant sight.'

When I arrived, the night duty inspector and a sergeant explained what they had discovered, after a panic call from a neighbour. The CID was on its way (which probably meant that they would have a lie-in while we secured the scene!).

It was a lovely house, small but comfortable; through a window, I could see colourful and imaginative decorations. The kitchen was cold but clean and tidy; trussed chicken in the oven, the door of which was open . . . vegetables prepared in saucepans. Everything seemed to be in order, until my eye fixed on a crumpled heap lying on the floor, half under the kitchen table. It was the mutilated body of a youngish woman.

I heard sobbing, sometimes howling, noises from another room where two children in pyjamas were with one of my policewomen. The kids were hiding their faces in cushions then lifting their heads and yelling. In another room, with a white-faced constable, was a whimpering man, making weird and hollow, eerie gurgling sounds and continually murmuring, 'I didn't mean it. I didn't mean it. It shouldn't have happened.' There was no sign of life from the woman in the kitchen; only a widening pool of blood coagulating on the floor.

Once I knew the whole story, following the husband's arrest, I had to feel so sorry for him. I wanted to step in and help but the law had to take its course. Weeks later, the hospital authorities and staff persuaded the Crown Prosecution Service that rather than punishment, he needed treatment and care. He was seriously mentally ill, a horribly disfigured and deranged young man through no fault of his own. He really did not know what he was doing.

What a dreadful memory of Christmas for those two young children. Would they, or could they, ever forgive their dad? What would happen to them if they couldn't or wouldn't? Would they endure years of bitterness and tortuous thoughts of revenge? Their lives were already blighted. Would they be completely destroyed? Or would there be room in their devastated hearts for some compassion for their clearly sick father?

Conclusion

The law, when infringed, provides a penalty, and law enforcers – police, solicitors, barristers, magistrates and judges – have an obligation to play their part. Common sense says that crime must be punished, and most people would applaud that – otherwise we would live in fear and trepidation.

As individuals, as I have found, even in the gravest situations, there is often room for compassion to grow – if we let it; but the question is, do we want it? As we read newspapers and listen to or watch the regular news programmes, I imagine that most of us are horrified when we are given details of crimes such as the soulless duping of the aged or abuse of children, to the point that any compassion for the perpetrators is far from our minds. However, as we explore the 'why' of forgiveness, especially when we, our family or friends are involved, we have to ask ourselves the question 'Do I *want* to forgive?' even before we meet the next question: '*Can* I?'

So, as we begin to explore the 'why' of forgiveness, I suggest we keep in mind that question – 'Do I want to?'

2

Isn't it natural?

'Let him rot in hell!'

'This is unforgivable.'

'Your life's worth nothing now – I'll get you!'

'That's it, you've crossed the line. There's no way back, never!'

So often, in scenes outside Courts and with the media in close attendance, we hear of families and friends who have been deeply hurt by tragedy – by a rape, for instance, or a paedophile taking a child, a murder; or something less extreme such as difficult neighbours – shouting these kind of sentiments to camera.

Years ago, when working as a sergeant in Soho, London, at the arrest of a gangland boss, he shouted to the open-mouthed onlookers, 'I always get my revenge. I insist on it!' I also heard from the evil mouth of a drug importer: 'I know who shopped me and she'll live in terror till I end her days.' And how many times have I heard this one: 'You're history!'

Gut feelings

These are gut feelings which you may think are only mouthed by those who are 'outlaws' or expressions breathed by those who have suffered greatly in the world I have policed. But you need to stop and think, just for a moment. We may never have actually uttered those oaths in public but haven't there been situations when we have *felt* like it? The feelings just seem to well up and are in our mind or even on our lips before we know it . . . Haven't we had the thoughts of retaliation, of 'it's not fair', of wanting to get our own back, of holding things against people, sometimes for *years*?

Try putting yourself in the position of parents whose young daughter has been raped and killed, or of a wife whose innocent husband has been shot in a bank raid, or of a young child whose parents have been killed in the family car by so-called 'joy riders' drunk or high on drugs in a vehicle they had just stolen. Try putting yourself in the place of a family whose elderly parents have been abused or neglected by staff in a local residential home, or in the heart of parents grieving over a son or daughter who is lying in a hospital Intensive Therapy Unit, fighting for life after overdosing on drugs sold by an inscrutable dealer.

Isn't it *natural* to hold grudges in such circumstances? Each of us is human after all and it *is* easier to want revenge, to hate, to hold a deep grudge than it is to forgive.

Having worked in inner-city London, Manchester, Bristol and Miami, I have heard the language of drug dealers who have been crossed or had their territory invaded by another gang; I have heard prison inmates who believe they have been 'grassed' or 'stitched up'; I've had to listen to the language of partners in failed marriages, fighting each other with no sense of remorse in front of their children – children who try to blot out the yelling by burying their heads under cushions. I have been called to schools where unrepentant bullies have continued to hurl abuse at teachers; I have tried to shut my ears at soccer matches, from local to Premiership levels, where abuse is screamed at the opposition or referees. In such scenarios, the F word is certainly not forgotten and that word it is *not* forgiveness.

Then there's 'road rage' – a driver fails to give way at a roundabout or junction; a driver overtakes without thinking; a driver who fails to dip headlights when driving closely behind another car . . . just a few examples of seemingly harmless incidents which trigger another driver to see red, wanting to take revenge, to intimidate, to teach them a lesson. But road rage that begins with retaliation often ends in a horrific accident, with serious injuries. Or there might be a furious fight between two drivers with the passengers getting involved too, with bloody results.

I was never in the Traffic Department but Steve often told me of incidents he'd witnessed on motorways, main roads, housing estates and so on. All too many ended in casualty wards – and some in the mortuary. It is *so* easy to get into the revenge game, often with disastrous consequences.

Explosive words

Having dealt with many explosive devices in central London during my Metropolitan Police career, I have experienced the strange atmosphere – the numbing effect, earth tremors and shockwaves, the horror, the carnage – when such a device explodes. Those who have fought in the front line in wartime (and any who have had bombs dropped on or near their property) will know exactly what I am saying. It is spooky, weird . . . I am talking of that moment immediately after the ear-shattering 'boom', before the debris and screams pierce the silence. That intense silence after an explosion is ghostly, a stunned silence, and *always* there is the fear, even an expectation, that there will be another blast.

Imagine, therefore, what it was like in November 1987 at the sombre Remembrance Day service held at the war memorial in Enniskillen, County Fermanagh, Northern Ireland when the solemnity was devastated by a deafening explosion. After the silence, there will have been some panic, injured people staggering away, some who were bewildered but bleeding where they fell and people lying dead – brutally killed by a home-made bomb.

The dust was settling, the emergency services were blue-lighting and wailing their presence, the security forces were nervously alert with their guns cocked; some of the screaming, shattered survivors were reeling around in a daze; blood was flowing in the gutters. What a scene from hell. Journalists were already seeking to gain what information they could, to write up their stories. But between the shouts, the screams, came the clear, lucid tones of Gordon Wilson, whose daughter was killed outright in the explosion. She was a nurse who might have been in the casualty department helping the injured.

'I forgive the bombers.'

Suddenly there was an eerie silence again; the ranks of the media and onlookers who would be baying for revenge, were stunned. Gordon, without any hesitation, in the middle of the carnage, was making this tear-jerking, emotional plea – 'forgive them' . . . One can only wonder how these cruel, heartless perpetrators of death would have reacted.

What an oasis from the more frequently heard 'Let them rot in hell' sentiments.

Some people would argue that such forgiveness is a sign of weakness . . . is it? Isn't it *normal* to want revenge

– to get even? And is it *right* to expect someone who has been deeply hurt, who may be inconsolable, to even *think* about forgiveness? To want revenge is perfectly natural . . . isn't it? To forgive, or even to think about, is surely against the natural order of things. Isn't that so?

Conclusion

These are reasonable questions but the bigger, much more pertinent, and even life-changing question is, 'What happens if we *don't* forgive, even in the most terrible circumstances?'

What happens to *us*?

Well, I can tell you. Holding on to hatred – even when it is perfectly understandable – clearly destroys just one person in the end.

The one who is doing the hating.

3

Consequences

Years ago, to reach the rank of Chief Officer in the police service required a successful six-month Senior Command Course at the National Police College, Bramshill; to be selected for that course meant a three-day ordeal in Eastbourne with sixty or so other senior officers competing for about a dozen places. In the midst of test papers, interviews, intelligence tests, 'chairing' meetings and so on was an hour-long session with a psychologist.

I was met in the hallway of the hotel by my interviewer. He shook my hand and then, as we walked towards his room, he said, casually, 'Do you think a convicted murderer can ever be ordained into the Christian ministry?'

Shutting the door behind me, I gave quick consideration to what I thought was merely an ice-breaker.

'Yes, I believe it's possible,' I replied.

'You really think that? What about the congregation? Surely they'd be in fear?'

'I see what you're getting at,' I admitted. 'But if anyone, however serious their crime, says sorry to God and turns from their sin, they can receive the forgiveness promised by Jesus. They can become a new person.'

The interviewer sat down. 'I can see you really believe that. But I'm also interested to discover if *people* – that is, congregations – can forgive a murderer.'

I smiled. 'Well, that's probably the crux of your original question. But it must depend on the congregation.' I could see he wanted me to go on, so I did. 'I wholly believe in the love of God through Christ who died. Christians should forgive too. But I do know that people can be very uncompromising. So while my answer to your question is a firm "Yes, a murderer can become an ordained minister" I ought to qualify that by saying that someone who has changed so much that they're a follower of Christ, may not get a congregation or local community to accept them. They may not be *willing* to have that person as their minister.'

The conversation continued on this theme throughout the hour we had together and the psychologist concluded the interview with one final question.

'Would you yourself forgive a convicted murderer if he had killed someone close to you?'

I gave him a short answer, perhaps not as firmly as I should have done – and little knowing that I would actually face this question in real life.

'Yes, I believe I would.'

Twenty years later, I did!

Bitterness

Harbouring bitterness, breathing threats against a perpetrator of death, never changes the one at whom we direct our hatred but it *does* change us – for the worse. A group of doctors was asked which emotions cause the most physical illnesses. Their answer was unanimous – 'anger and failing to forgive'. Countless numbers of mentally ill or stressed patients are in this category, their lives having been ruined by resentment, rancour, grudges and vindictiveness. The rehearsing of such emotions – the old hurts – drives their suffering even deeper.

What about parents who say they will never forgive when their son or daughter, having perhaps reached their late teens and turned to illicit drug-taking? What happens if that child leaves home and gets further into trouble and believes they can *never* go back? With the last words from their loved ones ringing in the ears: 'No forgiveness this time!' what is the incentive to return? What if real tragedy occurs then? Forgiveness *is* possible and presumably the parents would wish they had never said that they wouldn't forgive.

What if the child, at some stage, becomes completely drug-free, and yet believes the parents still won't forgive? What if the parents die before the addict child makes contact? The child could be wondering for the rest of their lives whether, if the parents had known of their transformation, they would have forgiven. The remorse, the grief, even the bitterness of rejection is intolerable all because of the failure to forgive at the right time.

Where there has been a hardness of heart, however understandable, a complete change of attitude, and communication of that change, must reach the child if there is to be reconciliation. Yes, there will be deep wounds to heal but *someone* has to make the first move. Supposing the child telephones home, Dad answers – and promptly hangs up? I have witnessed some heart-rending situations like this where only time-consuming persistence and diplomacy can bring the parties together . . . sometimes with a very happy ending.

I know a man – someone who has a bad past – who became a Christian. Having drifted away from his loving parents, their farm and his village, he turned to drink and was soon an alcoholic. Mixing with a crowd of low-lifes, he was soon into soft and then hard drugs. Being unemployed (perhaps even unemployable), he was then lured into petty theft. With convictions now part of his CV, he fell into violent crime and the stealing continued to pay for his drug habit. One day, he was with his cronies when someone was murdered and this man was stopped in his car by police . . . who discovered a body in his boot.

Later convicted of being an accessory to murder, he was sentenced to six years imprisonment. On his release, he fell into old ways, but he had a deep-seated longing to go back to his roots. After several unsuccessful attempts to change, he was eventually admitted to Ballyards Castle, a Christian rehabilitation centre in Northern Ireland. While drying out, he saw the care and concern of the staff and, on hearing the good news that God loved him and could change him on the inside and set him free, he put his trust in Jesus.

It was a hard, uphill struggle for him to re-establish his life and he had many set-backs. However, sometime later, he tried to seek reconciliation with his parents. Wonderfully, they had not entirely discarded him in their hearts – although they were very wary at first as to why he had come home. Still, after some weeks of spasmodic contact, his parents could see the evident change is their son's life; his lifestyle, his attitude was different. There were rumours that he'd become a Christian . . . He was gradually welcomed back into the family home and forgiven all the hurts that he had caused.

Very sadly, within a few months of his return, his mother was found to be seriously ill with cancer. His revolutionary change was evident as he spent hours at her bedside. She died with him beside her. The changed but distraught man was able to arrange the funeral and he read from the Scriptures in front of family and friends in the congregation. It was a testimony itself of what God can do; it's a fresh start: '. . . if anyone is in Christ, he is a new creation; the old has gone, the new has come!' (2 Cor. 5:17). The utter disappointment and despair when their son drifted away and was in trouble must have left a bitter taste for his parents. They would be thinking 'What did we do wrong?' and 'What could we have done to prevent this?' However, there was complete reconciliation which is, very sadly, not always the case.

If such a son is never welcomed back, the real victims are the parents who will be bound in resentment, blame, disappointment . . . and dented pride: 'How could *our* child have turned out like this?' Such parents may stand on their dignity, condemning a child and not receiving them back. Some neighbours and family would actually applaud this attitude.

Of course, it's quite normal for any parents in this situation to ask themselves questions about how such a downfall could have happened. Yes, there are always times when parents believe they could have done better in a particular situation with love, listening, encouragement and proper discipline. But by *not* keeping the door open for genuine repentance, however remote that possibility might seem, or by having a hard mind-set, it is possible to develop a sad and bitter heart. It is that attitude which can and does affect health. Even with an outward charade that all is well, underneath may fester a hatred of perceived failure. What follows is inconsolable depression, guilt, physical illness and a downward spiral of despair; we can't let it go, so it never lets us go.

The cure

Bitterness, of course, has many sources; the real and lasting cure is found in just one – forgiveness. The Bible is explicit: 'Keep a sharp eye out for weeds of bitter discontent. A thistle or two gone to seed can ruin a whole garden in no time' (Heb. 12:15, THE MESSAGE) and again, 'Make a clean break . . . Forgive one another as quickly and thoroughly as God in Christ forgave you' (Eph. 4:31,32, THE MESSAGE). How well we can see this enacted in biblical times, notably by Stephen, a Godly man in the early church, who was martyred, stoned to death. As he fell on his knees he cried out, 'Master, don't blame them for this sin' (Acts 7:60, THE MESSAGE).

Soon after our son's death in Manchester, a Salvation Army Captain asked the police to track me down. I telephoned him while I was staying with my daughter and her family in Altrincham. He told me that his son, too, had been killed by a terrorist – in Germany, some ten years before. The alleged murderer had been convicted and was still serving a long prison sentence. The Captain told me that he had been bitter ever since, always thinking what might have been and why should this happen to his son. In his heart he felt that a prison sentence was not sufficient punishment and he was always wanting some other sort of revenge. He told me that he certainly had never forgiven the terrorist.

However, he read in a newspaper that the father and family of a murdered police officer had openly and freely forgiven the terrorist in Manchester and that they were praying for the assassin. This moved the Captain. He had had no peace in his heart or ministry for all those years since his son died and now saw this opportunity to get right with God. He prayed, and forgave his son's killer unconditionally. Then, at last, he felt his heart and

mind at peace again. God had got through! What a mar-
vellous release from his self-inflicted prison; it was a
release which would transform his ministry.

Conclusion

Extreme circumstances always pose the question as to
whether such acts should be forgiven. Part of the problem is that most of us don't have to face such crises; our
failures to forgive are for much more trivial situations.
Harbouring bitterness and refusing to give someone a
second chance – this doesn't make room for any kind of
happy ending. And sometimes, just sometimes, happy
endings *are* possible.

So we'd do well to seriously consider the long-term
consequences when we won't forgive – both for ourselves and for our loved ones.

4

Blaming others

It's very easy to blame someone else when things go wrong, isn't it? Even when we are the ones at fault – or at least, partly at fault; this deflection of blame is often an attempt to turn away any embarrassment or punishment.

I'll let you into a secret. When police arrive at a simple damage-only accident or where there are very slight injuries, it is often the driver who is making the most noise and pointing the finger at others, who is actually at fault! OK, that's not always the case. But in my own experience, it has happened. I assume the guilty party thinks that by creating a big fuss it might divert the attention of a police officer. It doesn't.

Blame and claim

We live in an age where accusations are two a penny and where it is hoped that there may be some compensation. In my last years as Chief Constable, it was expected that there would be some claims against police officers simply because the government's retained insurance company would recommend a certain sum of money and settle a claim out of court rather than take the risk of a higher settlement plus the lawyer's fee and, maybe, costs too. I know of one case where a colleague wrote in his memoirs of Mr X who had committed a certain crime. Mr X was then awarded compensation because he said he did not commit the crime, but was *found guilty* of committing it. We have to be careful, don't we, of the exact words we use, in today's 'compensation climate'?

Matters that should never have attracted police attention are blown up out of all proportion. For example: imagine two neighbours with a boundary fence. One – we'll call him Mr S – causes some accidental damage to the fence. The neighbour – Mr T – runs next door and seriously assaults Mr S. Mr T is arrested. He is taken to court and fined. Then it escalates into claims and counter claims for further damage and injuries . . . if only Mr S had knocked on his neighbour's door and said, 'Sorry! I'll pay for the damage' and Mr T had said, 'Thanks. I'm sure we can sort it out.' This kind of attitude would save a lot of time, money – and stress.

Marriage breakdown is another sad area where parting seems to mean much more than divorce. Questions such as, 'What can I get out of it?' and 'How much can I prevent my spouse from getting?' are rife in the daily Family Courts. Of course, there *must* be an equitable settlement. But surely a polite, even amicable debate about finance and property is infinitely better than a long-running bitter dispute when assets are eaten into by legal costs and distraught children are caused yet more misery and anxiety. For often, unforgiveness, anger, and the 'blame and claim' culture don't just affect the people directly involved; the ripples are widespread.

In the medical world, I know that insurance premiums for some hospital staff, as for staff in GPs surgeries, have risen enormously because of the possibility of civil action when, for instance, there has been a mistake or some unforeseen deterioration following medical attention. Astronomical sums are paid out to aggrieved parties and I wonder whether this constant threat to consultants, surgeons, doctors and so on has any effect on *their* health.

Of course, I do fully recognise that there are some legitimate instances where someone has been hurt and, by going to court, justice is done. Some people even direct any money they are awarded to charity. Also, there are occasional cases where a plaintiff has won the case but been granted a small amount in damages yet been quite satisfied to have proved his point. However, generally speaking, where there is the possibility of getting rich, whatever the risks are before and during court hearings, an element of greed sneaks in. Forgiveness doesn't pay as well as retribution.

I'm not trying to throw cold water on people who deserve compensation and I'm certainly not in any way disparaging my fellow lawyers. But we live in a litigious society and what was once a last resort in seeking justice has become what I call the 'fruit machine syndrome' – put a little in to see how much we can get out. Blame someone and get rich.

But even when we don't stand to gain financially, it is so easy to point the finger at others – 'He did it' – especially when we know we might benefit out of the 'right' end result. I suspect we've all done it at some time in our lives, perhaps to avoid (justifiable) punishment. It takes a lot to forgive and say, 'Yes, you did it, but let's work it out between us' or even 'It was me. I'm sorry.'

Conclusion

We live in a 'blame and claim' culture. But let's remember that someone once said that when we point the finger at

someone else, we find three fingers pointing back at ourselves. So before we jump in and blame someone else –
even if we think we might gain something from doing so
– let's try to see the whole picture clearly. Why? Because if
we don't, we're likely to generate yet more bitterness and
misery for all concerned.

Blaming God

How many people, when in pain or other dire circumstances, call on God?

'Oh, my God!'

'Oh God, no!'

'God, help me!'

These are phrases which pour from the lips of Christian and non-Christian, especially when there's trouble.

I think society has changed considerably since my childhood and youth. In those days, a much larger proportion of people went to church albeit infrequently, and many had had experience of Sunday school. That is not the case today. There are those who only attend church at Christmas and Easter or for 'hatches, matches and despatches'; some will never enter a church building at all. For the most part, church-going is not a regular part of the majority of people's lives. More likely they will go to the local DIY store on a Sunday morning than attend any kind of worship service.

Of course, we often hear God's name invoked today by those who would assert that they have no belief whatsoever. How strange to think that his name is called upon probably more now than ever, but not out of a

sense of belief; I think relatively few would be ashamed
to be heard blaspheming.

I have had to get used to the expletives which are com-
monly used but I have never come to terms with those
who actually blame God for tragedy because I doubt that
those same people would rarely, if ever, thank him when
good things happen. Yet it is so easy to blame God when
things go wrong.

God was there

As I have already mentioned, the Sunday after Steve
died, we attended Poynton Baptist Church where he and
Lesley worshipped. The building was packed with its
normally large congregation, but swollen by some of
Steve's Special Branch colleagues, by neighbours who
wouldn't otherwise go to that church, by members of the
media and by a host of others, some of whom couldn't
get a seat. The morning service was not in any sense
mournful but had the exhilaration of worship with
songs, prayer and Bible-reading.

The minister, Rob White, asked several rhetorical questions, including, 'Where were you, God, when Steve died
last Tuesday?' Many might blame God for what happened;
others might say that God had deserted Steve otherwise he
wouldn't have permitted the tragedy to happen. But Rob
White answered his own question, 'God was right there
with Steve as he was wounded and as he died.'

God is not one who pinpoints people to hurt them, to
pull them down, to kill. Neither does he motivate people
to kill or maim others, or reward any killer who thinks
this is so. I don't blame God for what happened to Steve.
It has never even been a thought or temptation to accuse
God in any way. I know the character of God – good,

loving, faithful. God has promised his people that he will never leave them, that he will always be with them. His faithfulness is always assured. Yes, I believe God was there. Steve had not been neglected; Rob was right.

I wouldn't dare shake my fist at God and accuse him of wasting Steve's life. It would be unthinkable. I don't understand why it happened but I have learnt not to ask the unanswerable question 'Why?' and pray instead 'What now, Lord?' I recognise that God is with us in our grief and sorrow and that I still want to trust him and walk his way.

Obviously, not everyone feels like this when faced with terrible circumstances. But there is nothing special about me – the very opposite; I recognise God as my Father and accept his care and close attention. Yet many people see God as some distant mystical being with whom they have nothing to do, but when a crisis comes, it seems natural to shake a fist at him. That's why day after day, anywhere in the world, we might hear people accusing God of punishing someone because of a tragedy, or a business that's gone bust or even a sports team that has lost a crucial match. 'God, what have we done wrong that we deserve this?' or 'God, why me?'

He let me down . . .

Some years ago I was on duty in a police car and called to a block of flats in Paddington, west London. The call from Information Room, Scotland Yard, simply announced the address and concluded, 'Woman lying injured – ambulance on way.'

Arriving first, I saw a small but agitated crowd amongst parked cars within the inner courtyard of a huge block of apartments.

Someone called to me, 'She's over here.'

The starkness wasn't lost on me as the crowd parted and I, a lone police officer, walked through.

I saw the still figure of a middle-aged woman lying in a basement area. I knelt down beside her. She had blood on her clothing from a severe head-wound, and was bleeding from body injuries and fractures to both her legs. I felt a faint pulse.

I leant over her and said something like, 'An ambulance is coming . . . 'But she muttered very slowly and quietly so that I could hardly hear: 'Leave me alone, I want to die.'

I helped the ambulance crew to ease the injured woman onto a stretcher and up, over the railings into the ambulance. Sadly, she died before reaching hospital. I discovered from neighbours that she lived on the top floor, five storeys high, and I saw the open sash window from which two witnesses saw her jump.

The caretaker let me into her home so that I could try to trace her family. There, I found a scribbled note on the dining-room table:

> God has let me down. He has left me and now I can't stand living anymore.

Piecing together snippets of information, I believe that this woman had had a raw deal in life; estranged from her children, her husband had died of cancer fairly recently, and she had a potentially serious health problem of her own, yet to be investigated. She blamed God for her tragic circumstances.

I know that there are many people who are disillusioned about a life which may have given them a poor deal. I understand why they think that either God doesn't exist or that, if he does, he has left them to drown in their sorrows. But to believe God roams the world, every country, town, village or house looking to hurt people is to have a wrong concept of his character and nature. He longs for us all to trust him so that even when tragedy occurs, when things don't seem to be going our way, we can know that he is still actually there and in control. He can give physical and mental strength to cope, ability to face the crisis even through tears, disappointments, illness, bereavement and apparent disaster. Of course, Christians are not immune from tragedy, illness or accident, or troubles which are common to us all. But it is in the crisis that the Christian recognises the strength which comes from the living God.

. . . But did he really?

Sometimes we blame God when actually, we are in the wrong. We just don't realise it – or want to acknowledge it. Like the elderly man who called in to see his doctor at the local surgery.

'What's the problem?' said the doctor.

'It's my wife,' replied the old man. 'She has no idea how deaf she is. It's making me lose my temper all the time, I get so frustrated.'

'Get your wife to make an appointment to see me,' suggested the doctor. 'But before you do, to give me an idea of how deaf she is, go home and conduct an experiment.' The doctor then told the old man what he wanted him to do.

So the elderly man went home. Opening the front door, he called to his wife, 'I'm home! What's for dinner today?'

No reply from his wife in the kitchen.

He took another few steps and called again, 'What's for dinner, my love?'

Still no reply.

He repeated the question . . . nothing.

Then he came right next to her at the kitchen sink and said, 'What's for dinner today, darling?'

His wife looked at him, crossly. 'For the fourth time, I'm cooking sausages and bacon. Why don't you listen?'

The point of the story is that we may curse God and others, not recognising our own faults. God is cursed a thousand times a day by people who know nothing of his concern and compassion as if he is doling out 'punishment' to anyone he doesn't like or care about. Waving a fist at God is not only a complete and utter waste of time and energy – it also means that we may have bought the lie that he is someone other than who he really is.

Conclusion

Sometimes bad things that happen to us can be attributed to our own mistakes and wrong turns. But there are times, of course, where events and disasters strike that are manifestly *not* our fault. A sick child, a tsunami . . . still, some are eager to blame the Almighty for just about anything. My challenge to you is to find out for yourself what he is really like – for when we discover that, we will discover the reason why we really must move into an attitude of forgiveness. It follows that if anyone is blaming God for any crisis in their life, there can be little or no hope, certainly at that time, of accepting *his* love and forgiveness . . . then passing that on to others. Bitterness with God, as with any kind of bitterness, is a heavy weight to carry, isn't it?

6

The law and grace

We have already seen that the law does nothing to assist an offender; it cannot help that person back to a law-abiding life. Laws are guidelines and when laws are broken all that happens, like a mirror, is the reflection of guilt and condemnation. If enforced, the law punishes and then leaves the offender with little hope, for the law itself doesn't provide any kind of rehabilitation.

Law, in whatever shape or form, does not forgive, not forget nor give any strength or encouragement to the fallen. Rehabilitation law has been rightly welcomed but that only clears a record, not the conscience – and it cannot deal with future temptation. In short, the law or rules do not possess the power to help people on the 'straight and narrow'. It can condemn them for falling short but it cannot change the heart.

Law defines the boundaries of behaviour for ourselves and what we should expect from others. That is wholly laudable but, sadly, there are many who disregard it. So we see people stealing, defrauding, assaulting, committing sexual offences, taking illicit drugs, right down to, breaking speed limits and parking illegally!

We have also seen that it appears to be easier to be confrontational, argumentative and unforgiving than to live at peace with one another or at least to tolerate another's company – let's be honest: we find it's easier to do wrong than to do right, no matter how hard we try.

Introducing the bias

The truth is – we are born with a nature which is, as the Bible states so clearly, naturally sinful; that is, it inclines towards wrongdoing. Let me explain. For years, I had casually watched ladies and gentlemen play bowls. It seemed to be a quiet, leisurely game and, to the uninitiated, quite a simple one – rolling a black ball (called a wood) on grass to stop near a smaller jack. I soon learned that bowls is a game of great skill and tactics. The bowler must control the wood which is *weighted on one side* and needs to be steered in such a way that at certain speeds, it 'bends' towards the jack. Exactly like each wood on a bowling green, with its bias, we all without exception have a bias towards wrongdoing. We're born with it and our behaviour is affected from the very start of our lives. It contaminates our attitude, honesty and truthfulness; it invades our integrity, habits, thinking and planning.

Only one Person has ever been born and lived on the earth that did not have the bias towards sinfulness, inherited from our very first father, Adam, when he turned his back on God and chose to disobey him (see Gen. 3). This perfect individual is the man Jesus Christ. Why? He is unique in the history of humankind. He is God in a body, the Holy One: '. . . in Christ all the fulness of the Deity lives in bodily form' (Col. 2:9).

Just as we have laws to govern our land, so God gave humankind laws to live by. These are the Ten Commandments that God gave to Moses – we read about them in the Old Testament book of Exodus. But because of our inward bias, none of us is able to keep those laws. Yes, the law can show us where we go wrong; but it cannot help us to change our essential nature. Only Jesus could live a perfect life. We simply *cannot*. However hard we try, we can't fight the natural bias. Even the apostle Paul admitted this: 'When I want to do good, evil is right there with me. For in my inner being I delight in God's law; but I see another law at work in . . . my body' (Rom. 7:20-23).

God is holy. He is separate, other than us; as such, he cannot be tarnished by sin in the same way that he cannot tolerate sin. As with judgements we see reported in everyday life from Crown or Magistrates' courts, there is a penalty side to sin – it must be punished. Romans 6:23 says 'the wages of sin is death'.

Clearly, we can't save ourselves. And we certainly can't make ourselves right with God. We can never attain his perfect standard of holiness. There's a huge gulf between him and us – the law shows us that.

Left to our own devices, we are devoid of help. We are heading for punishment, justly deserved. As Paul cried out, 'What a wretched man I am! Who will rescue me from this body of death?' (Rom. 7:24). After all, if as Isaiah 64:6 says, 'all our righteous acts are like filthy rags', we are powerless to get right with God and live a life of victory over our bias. Aren't we?

The character of God

This is where it is crucial to know the character of God. For although we are naturally God's enemies, he is not ours. Listen to these words of Isaiah in the Old Testament.

> . . . he took up our infirmities and carried our sorrows . . .
> he was pierced for our transgressions and crushed for our
> iniquities; the punishment that brought us peace was upon
> him, and by his wounds we are healed. We all, like sheep,
> have gone astray, each of us has turned to his own way; and
> the LORD has laid on him the iniquity of us all (53:4–6).

This was God's Son, Jesus, the One who lived a perfect
and sinless life. And then laid it down for me and for you.
Only he could perfectly keep the law, for he had no sin in
him. Sin leads ultimately to death but the punishment for
our wrong actions, deeds and thoughts *has been taken by
Jesus* as he died in our place. Paul knew this; that's why
he could answer his own question, 'Who will rescue me?'
with the answer, 'Thanks be to God – through Jesus
Christ our Lord!' (Rom. 7:25). For although the wages of
sin is death, Romans 6:23 also assures us that 'the gift of
God is eternal life in Christ Jesus our Lord.' You may be
familiar with the famous verse in John's Gospel: 'For God
so loved the world that he gave his one and only Son, that
whoever believes in him shall not perish but have eternal
life' (3:16).

God's character and principle of forgiveness is per-
sonified in Jesus Christ, his Son. Not only in the works
that he did on earth (we will look at Jesus' attitude
regarding forgiveness in the next chapter) but crucially
in his death and resurrection. Such enormous cost, such
pain, such love for me and for you. *God gave* so that we
might be saved. This is who he is; we do not understand
how God can be Three and yet One, but we do know that
the Bible teaches this mystery. Jesus, God in a body, paid
the price because only he could. *This* is our God.

A good picture of how God loves us and longs to treat
every one of us, is seen in the famous story of the Prodigal
(or Lost) Son – although I prefer to call it 'The Gracious

Father'. The youngest son got fed up with home life on the farm and got from his father an early inheritance before running away and wasting all he had. But things went badly wrong and the son found himself poverty-stricken and as low as anyone could be. He decided to go home and ask for forgiveness. He had a well-rehearsed speech, not knowing how he would be received back, but before he could deliver it in its entirety, his father 'ran to his son, threw his arms around him and kissed him'. Then he threw a great party, so great was his joy that his son, who was dead, was alive again; he'd been lost, but was found (see Lk. 15). This is a stunning and effective picture of how God treats all who return to him.

Conclusion

We often think of the word 'grace' when we sit down for a meal. But grace actually means in this context God's free, unmerited, unearned favour. 'For it is by grace you have been saved, through faith – and this not from your-selves, it is the gift of God, not by works, so that no-one can boast' (Eph. 2:8,9). Perhaps, as we reflect on that, we can see another reason why we should forgive, too, and begin to understand why we should think about extend-ing *grace* to those who maybe we feel don't merit it.

7

Forgive us our debts . . .

We must never underestimate the deep cost that it was
for God to give his only Son to suffer so cruelly on the
cross so that our sin could be dealt with. Although forgiveness is free it is not cheap.

The Bible underlines time and again, there is no forgiveness without the shedding of blood. The Old
Testament pattern was that there would be a sacrifice of
an animal, its blood shed for the sins of the people. Sin is
serious; God doesn't treat it lightly, and neither should
we. Abraham's faith was tested when he was asked to
sacrifice his one and only son, the long-awaited Isaac.
The young boy asked his father, '. . . where is the lamb
for the burnt offering?' and Abraham's reply was that
'God himself will provide the lamb' (see Gen. 22:1–14).
John the Baptist introduced Jesus to the gathered crowd,
'Look, the Lamb of God, who takes away the sin of the
world!' (Jn. 1:29), and it was this same Jesus who three
years later hung on a cross, the sinless and perfect Son of
God, the Lamb of God, pouring out his blood for the sin
of the world. He was tortured and abused by the soldiers, betrayed by his own people, and jeered at by the
crowd and criminals alike. I suppose we might have
expected him to curse them all. But no: 'Father, forgive

them, for they do not know what they are doing' (Lk. 23:34). That's what he said.

God's whole nature is to love and be full of compassion. Scripture tells us 'The LORD is slow to anger, abounding in love and forgiving sin and rebellion' (Num. 14:18). The psalmist says 'he does not treat us as our sins deserve or repay us according to our iniquities' – why? 'For as high as the heavens are above the earth, so great is his love for those who fear him' (Ps. 103:10,11). And yet sin must be punished – and of course, we have already seen that the punishment has fallen on God himself, in the Person of his Son.

In the book of Exodus, we read of the instigation of the Jewish Passover. If you are not familiar with the story, you can read it in chapter 12. The Israelites were in slavery in Egypt, and God was setting them free. But because the Pharaoh would not let the Israelites go, terrible plagues were being visited on the land. Finally, the angel of death was going to be sent to take out all of the firstborn. But God told the Israelites to take a lamb for the Passover meal, and anoint the tops and sides of the doorframes of their homes with the blood – 'when I see the blood, I will pass over you' (v. 13). They were safe, the angel of death didn't touch them . . . and they were set free from their bondage. We might think this a frightening picture, but actually it speaks of Jesus. He is our Passover lamb. His shed blood means judgement *passes over* us. Why? Because Jesus has paid the price; he *loves* us.

The ministry of Jesus

That forgiving heart of God is so clearly seen in the ministry of Jesus. His power to forgive sins and willingness to do so is seen in the example of his heal-ing the paralytic man. Jesus not only dealt with his paralysis but forgave him too (Mk. 2:1–12). Again, we see this forgiveness when an acrimonious group, trying to test Jesus, pointed to a woman caught in adultery. Jesus calmly said to the crowd, 'If any one of you is without sin, let him be the first to throw a stone at her.' Hearing that, the accusers walked away. The woman was left with Jesus. He said, 'Woman, where are they? Has no one condemned you?' She replied, 'No one, sir.' And then Jesus told her, 'Then neither do I condemn you.' But he added, 'Go now and leave your life of sin' (See Jn. 8:1–11). The Gospels are full of examples of Jesus' forgiving attitude. Ever heard of the tax collector, Zaccheus? We can read about him in Luke 19:1–11. Unlike me, he was a very little man so he had to climb a tree just to see Jesus as he walked by. Tax collectors of that day were despised for their dishonesty and extor-tion and for that reason they were shunned in society. Zaccheus was no exception, as he admitted (see Luke 19:1–11).

Jesus saw him, called him down and said he was going to stay at the tax collector's house. The crowd murmured about Jesus going off to be the guest of a man like that. And then something amazing happened. Zaccheus said, 'Look, Lord! Here and now I give half of my possessions to the poor, and if I have cheated any-body out of anything, I will pay back four times the amount.' Here was forgiveness without any strings attached – no limits, no qualification. And here was a man who was honest with himself, not trying to justify his actions and therefore honest with God. Zaccheus was forgiven, and restored to a right relationship with God; a heart change had happened, as was apparent by his actions as he 'got right' with others too.

Forgiveness begins with God

So because of God's unconditional love, we can be forgiven, and we can know true restoration with God and others. We can see that forgiveness begins with God. We don't get what we deserve – because of his love. God's character reveals that he is not only compassionate and forgiving by nature but that, to anyone who listens, he *promises* to forgive and forget. We read in Hebrews 8:12: 'I will forgive' but also 'I will remember their sin no more.' But one of the very sad things about life is that we have long memories. Earlier, we read about Jesus' story of the Lost Son. It is interesting to see how the boy's older brother was not so welcoming. He resented what his father said and did and had no compassion in his heart for his brother's repentance and restoration. All too often, we are like that brother.

We may well forgive someone who has wronged us but then we keep reminding them and ourselves of what they did. Years later, it is recounted and held against them. God very deliberately doesn't do that – once forgiven never remembered.

Jesus showed by example how he expects us to treat our enemies: 'Love your enemies and pray for those who persecute you' (Mt. 5:44). And of course, he gave us the well-known prayer known as the Lord's Prayer (see Mt. 6:9–13):

> Our Father in heaven,
>   hallowed be your name . . .
> Forgive us our debts,
>   As we also have forgiven our debtors.

Whichever translation is used, this is a two-part sentence, one dependent on the other. What is so frequently ignored is the emphasis that the Lord Jesus put on these words – we must forgive. Why? So that we might be forgiven. 'For if you forgive men when they sin against you, your heavenly Father will also forgive you. But if you do not forgive men their sins, your Father will not forgive your sins' (Mt. 6:14,15). So to be forgiven, we must forgive.

In Romans we read: '. . . if you see your enemy hungry, go buy that person lunch, or if he's thirsty, get him a drink. Your generosity will surprise him with goodness. Don't let evil get the best of you; get the best of evil by doing good' (Rom. 12:20,21, THE MESSAGE). But that's not always easy, is it?

Conclusion

In this section, we have explored reasons *why* we must forgive. But what if we simply *can't* forgive? Do we think we will be letting the one who hurt us 'off the hook'? Remember, God forgives, but he also punishes sin that is unrepented – 'It is mine to avenge; I will repay' (Rom. 12:19). By forgiving our enemies, as Jesus commands, we are not letting them off the hook; we are in effect letting *ourselves* off the hook. But still, we may feel we do not know *how* to do it.

That's what we will look at next.

PART 3

Forgiveness – How?

INTRODUCTION: Help!

When we believe in Jesus and ask him to forgive us for our sins – when we have, in effect, seen that the huge price he paid on the cross of Calvary was for us as individuals – he forgives us and we start a whole new life in him. The Bible calls it being 'born from above' or 'born again' (see Jn. 3:3–7). We become 'new creations' in Christ (2 Cor. 5:17). The power to live for Jesus is imparted to us by his Spirit, living in us. That isn't to say, though, that we won't go wrong and let Jesus down – again and again.

Jesus on earth was tempted like we are. But the huge difference between Jesus and us is that *he never yielded to temptation*. He knows what it is to have the pressure of being lured away from the right path by the influence of sin – but he never once caved in.

So the problem of 'doing wrong' is still around even when we put our trust in Jesus and decide to follow him. Why? Because our old nature, the built-in bias, still rises up within us. We are tempted, often unconsciously, and still have the vulnerability to fall. The apostle Paul put it like this

I do not understand what I do. For what I want to do I do not do, but what I hate I do. And if I do what I do not want to do, I agree that the law is good. . . . I know that nothing good lives in me, that is, in my sinful nature. For I have the desire to do what is good, but I cannot carry it out. For what I do is not the good I want to do; no, the evil I do not want to do – this I keep on doing. Now, if I do what I do not want to do, it is no longer I who do it, but it is sin living in me that does it. So I find this law at work: When I want to do good, evil is right there with me. For in my inner being I delight in God's law; but I see another law at work in the members of my body, waging war against the law of my mind and making me a prisoner of the law of sin at work within my members (Rom. 7:15–23).

But there's good news! When we fail, the wonderful thing is that Jesus will forgive us again and again and again. Of course, the law doesn't allow for such unconditional mercy. But grace does. Yes, there will be struggles. But in Jesus, our lives can be guided in the right path, so while that natural bias still kicks in, we are much more aware of life's temptations and pitfalls.

The Bible teaches that there is no limit to God's patience and forgiveness; if anything, when we recognise our sin, it is we who feel that our failure must undermine his love for us.

The closer we come to Christ, the more we see our own faults, weaknesses and failings. We might ask ourselves, 'What's the point? I'm a failure' when we habitually sin and constantly seek his forgiveness and renewal. But although we may stumble, and occasionally we may fall, Jesus understands our weaknesses (see Heb. 4:15,16) and is able to pick us up so we can begin to walk again. He came to give us life above the ordinary, a forgiven life, a renewed life through his Spirit. As anyone who trusts the Lord knows, a deep strength is given, a peace at heart and mind is experienced and, incredibly, it is then possible to walk in his way and have the attitude of Christ himself.

So if you are asking, 'But *how* can I forgive?' read on; for Jesus is all too willing to help us to live to please him – and that includes *forgiving as he has forgiven us* . . . through his power.

1

A good example

I was the superintendent in charge of the Moss Side sub-
division in South Manchester. It was a volatile area but
most of the residents were hardworking, very hos-
pitable, full of fun, with happy families. It was a mixed
community of Afro-Caribbean and Asian origins which
easily dovetailed with an indigenous Mancunian popu-
lation.

Many, indeed most, residents in the district went out of
their way to befriend my colleagues and me. We spent
time with them in their homes, churches, mosques, tem-
ples and at schools and in the parks, or just walking the
streets. There was a lot of joviality, sensible conversation
and, perhaps most pertinent, hope for the future – especially for the young people. Most of them, as families,
enjoyed their lifestyle despite in some cases being on the
poverty line. They did things together – they laughed and
cried together. Generally, as a community, I found that the
one thing which they disliked was being patronised by
some politicians or imported groups trying to give mean-
ing to their lives. They didn't like being in the spotlight.

Sadly, permeating this placid and happy amiability
were undercurrents of unrest. There was a friction
because of the illicit drug-dealing and drug abuse – and

the associated crimes of theft and violence – amongst a very small minority. There was a definite problem with a few troublemakers who did their utmost to ferment bad feeling between each of the cultures. It was very intimidating to the law-abiding and upright people who lived there. Such troublemakers, generally, were not resident in Moss Side, Hulme, Chorlton, Longsight or Withington but had infiltrated the area from elsewhere. The racism which resulted – by verbal insults and obscene graffiti – was generally ignored and treated with contempt but sadly it gave the place a bad name.

A terrifying night

Following widely reported riots in Toxteth (Liverpool), Bradford, Southall and in Birmingham, it didn't take much to light the fuse in Moss Side. Some of the troublemakers were quietly stirring the emotions of a few young people. There were indications that something was very wrong when the local youth clubs began buying an unusual number of baseball bats . . . And then milkmen started complaining that there were fewer empty bottles to collect than usual (bottles are used for making petrol bombs).

Soon after an anti-drugs operation on the outskirts of the area, the excuse had been created to copycat the rioting elsewhere in the country. This began in the early hours of a July morning. Fires were deliberately started in some shops in scattered locations. This put the Fire Brigade under enormous pressure and, as if that were not enough, the fire officers were being stoned as they played their hoses on the flames.

Police were doing their best to protect their fire-fighting colleagues and that gave space for all hell to let loose.

I will never forget when the police station was stormed. The few of us trapped inside endured a terrifying night as petrol bombs slammed into the building; windows were stoned and smashed and we had to keep shoring them up. That night we watched the fires blazing amongst vehicles parked in the yard and had to listen to eerie chanting and animal noises that chilled the blood. It was a terrifying experience not only for the dozen or so of us inside the wrecked building but for the many neighbours in the flats immediately next door. Still, we were able to repel the attackers who were trying to climb in through smashed ground-floor windows. And, incredibly, what injuries there were seemed to be superficial.

Outbreaks of violence and damage continued for four days and nights. This inevitably threw an unnecessary spotlight on policing. Blame was shouldered – perhaps unwillingly because most of it was completely unjustified – by me as the man in charge. The majority of the local residents recognised, however, that we were just trying to blend with the community whatever race, colour, creed or religion, and rid the area of its crime. Some began to voice their support to the Police Committee, to the subsequent Enquiry and to my colleagues as they continued their good work on the streets. Contempt was loudly expressed for the rioters, who represented very few of the decent people of all backgrounds in the area. Yes, there were lessons to be learnt by all sides but violence and revenge were not the answer.

I was glad to hear the eventual outcome of the reports, and adjust our plans and community activities where necessary. But my personal aim was to change the bad image that was now hanging like a fog over the area and streets of Moss Side. It meant facing a lot of questions at public meetings, in the Police Committee, at the official

Enquiry but not least from the local Ministers' Fraternal. I had received a rather terse 'invitation' (it was more of a directive actually) to meet with these churchmen and women, and I arrived a little early so as not to offend them in any way. Unfortunately, with no one to greet me, I overheard them debating whether they should open the meeting in prayer because a police officer was attending. They voted not to!

The praying begins

I came away rather disappointed and subdued. I'd hoped there might have been a measure of understanding from fellow Christians but I believed there was no thought of forgiveness or reconciliation there.

Then I received a phone call in my office from Father Leigh, a local Roman Catholic priest who I hardly knew but who subsequently became a great friend and ally.

'Mr Oake,' he started, 'I was at the meeting this morning and could have wept for you, knowing what you have been trying to do in the neighbourhood. I believe we both know the root cause of the unrest. I wonder if you would meet with me and three of my colleagues. We'd like to talk with you, pray for new things in Moss Side and plan with you. Can we meet in your office?'

Out of that afternoon came some wonderful new things. Firstly, it was that group which suggested changing the name of the police station to Greenheys – which the Chief Constable and the Police Committee wholeheartedly endorsed. Also, I was asked to preach in their respective churches and have the services advertised widely that a police officer was participating. This was, of course, a slight risk; it was a daunting task as there could have been demonstrations and mud-slinging at each venue but that never happened and I was well received.

Out of that group came the phoenix, as we called it; the burnt-out premises of the Roberts' Cycle Shop became the hub of Moss Side. With much local help, including young people, as well as professional services for building work, decorating, plumbing and so on, the 'shell' was refurbished into a meeting place with coffee, tea and soft drinks being served all day and a second-hand swap-shop; there were two rooms for sleeping accommodation and a quiet room. It was named 'The Open Door' and staffed by volunteers and at least one constable during opening hours – that was in my day, and may be still happening. A popular centre for Moss Side.

I had let the group know that I wanted to spend time with three men who were community leaders. Sadly, although I visited one in hospital where he was suffering from cancer, he died before we had any sort of rapport; another agreed to meet me in a spare room behind a doctor's surgery – out of the district. These were helpful and healthy meetings with Hartley Handley.

Charlie Moore

The third leader I couldn't seem to get near. This was a man named Charlie Moore. He avoided all attempts to meet me. Then, I heard through the grapevine, that he had become a Christian! Wonderfully, through the prayer and encouragement of his secretary at Moss Side Youth Club, Charlie had started to attend church. It wasn't long before he began following Christ.

One day, while sitting in my office at Greenheys, the telephone rang to announce that Charlie Moore was at the front counter asking to speak with me.

'Would you like someone to be with you?' asked the sergeant. 'I'll get the Duty Officer to come in.'

'No,' I said, 'I'll come down and bring him up to my office. We'll be alone.'

'Sir, is that wise?' the sergeant was concerned now. 'You know he was behind the riots!'

'Yes, I know and I want to meet him,' I replied. 'Alone, please.'

So I went to the counter and put out my hand to Charlie. He shook it.

I invited him upstairs into my office, asked for a tray of tea and said, 'I hear good things about you, Charlie. What's happened?'

'I've changed,' he said. 'I'm a Christian now.' He shifted awkwardly. 'Look, I'm very nervous about this. But I've come to say sorry about my behaviour, the incitement and the riots.'

He became very tearful; I could see he was serious and genuine as he told me about how he came to faith in Jesus. His past had caught up with him. He had so many regrets but recognised that Jesus had died for him and he could be forgiven.

When he'd finished, I stood up.

'Have you ever hugged a honkey?' I said. 'Come here.'

And we hugged till it hurt – a big, beefy Afro-Caribbean and an equally big British white man.

I hadn't seen Bob, my clerk, come in with the tea. I rather suspect he was shaken to the core to see the perpetrator of Moss Side riots in a clinch with me. *That* soon got round the station.

Then Charlie looked at me and very shyly asked, 'Can you forgive me?'

I remember my reply as if it were yesterday: 'I never thought this day would come. Charlie, you've been given new life as a Christian. You're forgiven by God and now by me. Of *course* I forgive you.'

Charlie joined the group which was still regularly meeting in my office and because he was so well known and respected by many young people, was a real motivator in rebuilding Moss Side. Later, when I was preaching at one of the 'black' churches, Charlie introduced me to three of the lads who were leaders in attacking the police station. Each had also started going to church through Charlie's encouragement . . . though, I have to say, they were very nervous about meeting me.

So you can see from this story, miracles can happen. Because of Jesus, we *can* forgive – and be forgiven. Christ can change people by his power, whereas we cannot change ourselves any more than we can make ourselves 'right' with God.

This account of Charlie and me is exactly how it happened in Moss Side. The new look and exciting attitudes of the district accelerated because of this. We had wonderful encouragements from Manchester City Football Club when players and coaches took sessions on their practice pitch with the kids, as well as finding renewed vigour within 'religious' and non-religious people, those working in social issues, counsellors, politicians . . . all these were ready to seek change and repair.

The real heroes in all that were not those calling the police to task, or criticising Chief Constable Jim Anderton who used to pay regular visits and spend time listening to residents and their families; neither were the heroes the 'do gooders' who tried to return to what Moss Side used to be and thus were not even trying to seek reparation or look to the future.

He didn't want any recognition but Charlie Moore found not religion but a personal and life-changing relationship with Jesus Christ. He was a forgiven man by God

and then he asked us to forgive him and that began something wholly new. And neither did the group who met in
my office seek praise; but they, by prayer and planning,
discovered that even from the direst of circumstances,
new life can spring up again. It wasn't about heroes at all;
the open secret was in the words of Jesus: 'Forgive us our
debts, as we also have forgiven our debtors.'

Charlie and I spent much time together. One day he
said, 'Robin, please tell me again that you forgive me. I
am so sorry to have blamed the police.' Then he added,
'And if they did do wrong, if you have done wrong, I forgive you on behalf of the youth of Moss Side.'

'Charlie Moore,' I said, 'thank you. Yes, as the boss, I
forgive you and you must take my word for it. But you're
right. I also need your forgiveness and understanding if
we've done wrong and hurt you and your lads.'

He simply looked me in the eye and said 'Done!' with
a high five.

It was the beginning of a solid friendship. After I came
to the Isle of Man, I invited Charlie to our home and he
brought with him eight young ladies from his church to
sing at various locations on the Island (and also to participate in the national netball tournament which they
won!). Is there no limit to what God can do? No. Because
it's all about his power – not ours. And when we really
see that, we will understand that change in others and
ourselves is not impossible. It *is* possible to forgive and
be forgiven – even in the unlikeliest situations with the
unlikeliest people!

Conclusion

Before we can get into the business of forgiving others,
we need to really make sure we have seen our own need

for forgiveness and change – and to realise that we cannot change ourselves. For it is only when we see, like Charlie did, that we need help, that we can reach out to Jesus and receive it.

When we receive his forgiveness, the next step is to reach out to others and extend to them what we have received ourselves; Charlie asked for forgiveness, but he was then able to extend forgiveness to those who had hurt him. So next, let's look at the basis of forgiveness – being forgiven. In other words, the need to own up.

2

Owning up

To be forgiven, first of all, we need to recognise what is not right with us and also where we have gone wrong in our lives. So we ought to be honest and recognise that we are not unique, we have all been born with that built-in bias towards wrong that we have already talked about.

There is no shame in that because it is common to all humankind whoever we are, whatever our status. No matter how sophisticated we think we are or how well educated we have been or how bright we assess ourselves to be, how wealthy or how poor we are, that bias has spoilt the best of family lines and contaminated royalty, nobility and everyone else. It is irrelevant whether we have what can be described as a good upbringing in a stable family or whether we have no idea who our father is. The bias away from good is common to all people and therefore since we cannot control ourselves or 'pull ourselves up by our boot laces', we need to be in the right hands if we have any sort of desire to be better, to have life to the full. I am sure you realise by now that those 'right hands' are the hands of Jesus.

How dare you!

Ron Perrett, a good friend and a fellow police officer, was my best man when I married Chris. A powerful speaker, he was at a local venue, Mint Walk in Croydon, Surrey, where he was addressing a men's group, speaking on 'What's your Life?'

It had been a formal evening where others had been participating, with Ron as the final speaker. Members of that mission had taken the opportunity to invite friends and colleagues to hear him so it was a large and very mixed audience.

As Ron spoke of his wartime experiences in World War Two on the front line in North Africa and Sicily, he mentioned his near-death experience when advancing north in Italy; he was a radio-communications corporal in the turret as his tank received a direct hit from a German shell. Severely injured, he regained consciousness while being flown back to England but had months of painful treatment before his full rehabilitation.

He continued to speak about joining the Metropolitan Police following his Army discharge and his varying experiences in central London's 'A' Division. He emphasised the strength of his Christian faith even through these experiences. Ron went on to translate the evils of warfare and his policing of offenders to personalise the fact that, as the Bible says, we have *all* sinned and come short of God's perfect standard (see Rom. 3:23). At this there was some shuffling in the audience, with men looking at one another.

Then, as if it were a board meeting, a middle-aged man stood up and said to Ron, while he was in full flow: 'I challenge that. I'm not what you call a sinner. How dare you!'

Another man rose to his feet across the room and simply said, accompanied by a lot of indignant murmuring,

'I second that' as if they were about to vote on and settle the issue! Had Ron stopped speaking there and then, those men might well have had a majority declaring they were sinless. Ron doubts if many of his audience would have agreed with *him* – but of course, they were actually denying the truth of the Bible.

I am sure that each of us could justify ourselves and the way we live, condoning many of the things we have done wrong. We might say, as we compare ourselves with others, 'I'm not too bad, really.' But it is when we look at *God's* standard, as Ron was doing, that if we are honest, we have to concede that the inbuilt bias kicks in far too often and constantly reveals itself to us as our naturally sinful nature.

Admit it!

To begin the road of being forgiven means genuine openness and honesty – being frank as we recognise the awful fact of sin in our life. Only then can we confess that sin to the One who can do something about it. It is said that confession is good for the soul and there is a good deal of truth in this. Children take a long time to learn that owning up is actually far better than deceitfulness. However many times have we, as children, heard our parents call out, 'Who did this?' While the immediate consequences of saying 'It was me' seem to be well out of proportion, it is actually far better in the long run to say, 'I did it' rather than stay silent – or worse, say 'It wasn't me. *She* did it!'

Honesty is the best policy – with God and with ourselves. The Bible is quite clear, as I am sure my friend Ron pointed out to his audience:

If we claim that we're free of sin, we're only fooling ourselves. A claim like that is errant nonsense. On the other hand, if we admit our sins – make a clean breast of them – God won't let us down; he'll be true to himself. He'll forgive our sins and purge us of all wrong-doing. If we claim that we've never sinned, we out and out contradict God – make a liar out of him. A claim like that only shows off our ignorance of God' (1 Jn. 1:8-10, THE MESSAGE).

Admitting our sin is the all-important first step. It's not always easy because we are naturally proud people and certainly don't willingly open ourselves up to others to allow them to see that we are not really up to scratch. We may feel it is beneath our dignity to admit failure and, anyway, by whose standards are we saying that we *sin*? Sometimes we need to take a good long look at God's standards to see that our own really do fall short.

Admitting sin, then, is the first step, but it's a big one. An alcoholic, or indeed, a drug addict, seeking a first step to kick the habit and to seek reformation, has to admit dependence before anything else can happen. There is no first step until that acknowledgement is made – that is, to themselves and then to a counsellor. It is also part of the healing process (maybe the hardest part) to be open with fellow addicts in group work and admit the problem fully.

When we recognise that this is the essential first step as far as sin in our life is concerned, then we are beginning to get in tune with our heavenly Father. The Bible tells us 'all have sinned and fall short of the glory of God' (Rom. 3:23). It is an inescapable fact. The big problem is that until the bias is taken in hand, our basic nature is in control and although it doesn't make us all criminals, life at its very best is just not achievable, for all our trying and striving.

So until we own up to our own personal bias towards sin and can be absolutely truthful with ourselves, we will continually fall short of God's standard. And until we admit our essential flaw, we cannot be honest with God so we have no hope of receiving his forgiveness. If we can't believe that we are contaminated by this sinful nature, what is there to forgive?

However, when we *do* see it, we agree with our great God. And then we can begin to do something about it. Seeking from our Saviour forgiveness and cleansing from the nature we have inherited, we begin again by receiving the Spirit of God. The change does not come by keeping New Year resolutions, by church attendance, by turning over a new leaf, by meeting targets which we set ourselves, by eastern meditation or by anything else except to God through Jesus his Son – all else is doomed to failure. For 'Salvation is found in no-one else . . . there is no other name under heaven given . . . by which we must be saved' (Acts 4:12). Jesus said he was *the* way to God, not *a* way (see Jn. 14:6). When we come to Christ we receive *his* righteousness, holiness and redemption (see 1 Cor. 1:30). We have to believe Jesus can save us – step two.

This is not 'becoming religious' but starting a new relationship. God knows what we are like and also knows how wise and releasing it is not only to admit our sin but to take the next step of confessing it. We will find some liberation – like being relieved of a sack of manure on our backs – when we make a clean breast of things to a particularly close friend or to a counsellor. When we are honest to God and confess to Jesus, he begins a healing process. There is no penance or forfeit – nowhere does God demand self-flagellation or any punishment devised by humanity; we must just *receive* his forgiveness and cleansing and depend upon him to do it, which is the next step.

So, we will know a complete renewal, for to all intents and purposes we begin a new life – we are 'born again'

– a new heart, a new spirit; we give to Jesus the 'old me' and we get a 'new me'. And this is for eternity! We can know the assurance of that. Missionary Jim Elliot, when challenged about his faith, said: 'He is no fool who gives up what he cannot keep to gain what he cannot lose.' We can't hold on to life for more than the few decades we live on this earth. We must recognise that and let go so that we may gain eternal life in Christ; for when we trust him, Jesus not only forgives us and gives us a fresh start; he gives us a new life that no one can *ever* take away.

Self-forgiveness

There is another issue to face which I would not wish to ignore at this point, or only give casual attention to. That is *self*-forgiveness. You'll never guess the number of times I have heard people say to me, to a court or to the media, 'I'll never forgive myself' or 'What I've done is unforgivable.' Yes, as a police officer, I have come across some abhorrent things that one person has done to another or said about someone else and I am certain that all of us have done things of which we are deeply ashamed and will always regret. But while this senti-ment is quite understandable and very common, there has to be a way of escape. Sadly, some people have not been able to deal with such memories and have sunk fur-ther into the mire of regret and shame. Some believe that self-harm or suicide is a way of penance to show the other party or society the remorse which they feel. There will be no real healing unless we properly deal with our memories and with what we have done that we regret. And while confession is important here, we must also not allow ourselves to wallow in the past.

The famous composer Mozart, as most will know, was a child protégé and, as he grew to maturity, his performances at the piano and his compositions were renowned throughout Europe. However, one man regretted the attention Mozart was receiving in contemporary society; that was Salieri, himself a composer of great talent. Mozart was outshining him not just by his published and performed works but also in popularity. This made Salieri so bitterly envious that he began to secretly plot what he hoped would be Mozart's downfall. Recorded (maybe a little inaccurately) in the film *Amadeus*, it led to a life of evil intent, misery and ultimately incarceration in a lunatic asylum. Instead of seeing Mozart as a genius to be admired, Salieri saw him as a rival and by so doing, completely ruined his own abilities and appreciation of good music. He never forgave Mozart his accomplishments, his abilities, his plaudits but by this omission, destroyed his own potential, his health and finally his life.

More recently, it was reported from America that a man in his mid-thirties, with a wife and three children, had remorse for his secret abuse of children twenty years before and had borne the guilt of that ever since. In his suicide note, addressed to his unsuspecting wife, he referred to that and the premature death of one of his daughters. He said he was filled with so much hate towards himself and God, and unimaginable emptiness; he said he went right back to anger.

It was reported by the press that the guilt and stress wore him down to an unbearable breaking point which drove him to a small school in the Amish Community in Pennsylvania where he shot several girls before turning the gun on himself. If only he'd unburdened himself to someone, even his wife, and repented towards God, this tragedy may never have happened. But what emerged from this dreadful tragedy was that this Christian community made it known that they had forgiven the killer. They invited his widow and children to the funerals of those who had been murdered.

The widow then wrote an open letter to the Amish Community that their love for her family had helped provide healing; the Amish's compassion had reached beyond the killer's family and community, and was changing their world.

Remorse is necessary when we have done wrong but unreleased self-deprecation is so harmful. This is why there is a real demand for counsellors – counsellors are people whose primary gift is to be a good listener. They hear the problem, share the burden and release the 'stopper' of guilt. And of course there are family and friends and those within local churches who have the gift of listening, too; they can also pray.

The highest and best listener is Jesus Christ himself. Firstly, there is no time when he is not listening and secondly, 'there is now no condemnation' (Rom. 8:1) from him. No matter how badly we feel, we can offload to him and find forgiveness. Jesus said, 'Are you tired? Worn out? Burned out . . .? Come to me. Get away with me and you'll recover your life. I'll show you how to take a real rest. Walk with me and work with me . . .' (Mt. 11:28,29, THE MESSAGE). So, do it!

Conclusion

Owning up isn't easy, but it's essential if we want to move into good things with God. I find the steps we've covered in this chapter helpful when put in this way.

We must

A – *admit* our bias and acknowledge the sin that comes from that and keeps us separated from the God of real life

B – *believe* that Jesus can forgive the sin and that we can be open with him

C – *confess* the sin and receive his cleansing

D – *depend* on him to hear our prayer and to cleanse us

E – believe that we have *eternal life* when we follow Christ for he has

F – *forgiven* us and

G – *given* us a new start.

3

Forgiveness and restoration

We may believe God will forgive us, and we can even forgive ourselves. But what about seeking the forgiveness of others? When we realise that we have done something wrong, or said something we regret, or hurt another in some way, how do we gain their forgiveness?

Can we ask directly: 'Do you forgive me?' If so, aren't we putting the offended person in a corner? And isn't the most likely response a rebuff? What do we do if they say to us, 'Forgive you? No, I don't!'?

Come clean!

When seeking God's forgiveness, we have to admit our sin; it is always necessary for us to 'come clean'. It's the same when we are dealing with others. It's not an easy path to take; in seeking to get right with a friend, a neighbour, a colleague or anyone else, we have to come to terms with admitting we are wrong. We have to think about saying something like, 'Look, I know I was wrong the other day. I am so sorry. I know I've hurt you and I want you to know just how much I regret it.'

If we can't face a person or even phone them, we may be able to write a letter, email or text a message. This is not necessarily a 'coward's way out' because it does give time to think through what should be said; there is an opportunity to make a draft and alter something which, on second thoughts, could be better phrased. The other advantage is that it gives time for the recipient to read through the communication more than once before responding.

I think, though, in real life it is rarely the right thing to actually *ask* the offended person for their forgiveness. It may happen in films or plays and add to the tension and drama. But I believe it is putting out a wrong message to ask for *anything* when we have offended someone – let alone their forgiveness. What we can and should do, after having spoken to that person or written to them, is to earnestly pray that our regret and sorrow will be seen as deeply sincere and that somehow, we might be forgiven in time.

We can so easily wound others in small ways. In the home, where we live closely together, it is easy to have a sharp tongue when we are tired or feeling unwell. We may say things which we immediately regret, or do something deceitfully or lie about something. Things said and done in the heat of the moment can create a terrible atmosphere. So often, tension and arguments are initiated simply because of criticism.

I was once called to settle an argument in what seemed to be a well-kept and amiable home. But the man's partner was grieved because she wasn't being appreciated for her housework and so on; in fact, the man had accused her of 'ironing in tram lines on a trouser leg when pressing the clothes'. It not only created a scene it caused such a rumpus that neighbours called the police to sort it out!

The advice my wife and I were given at the start of our married life was to 'keep accounts short'. Apologising is never easy but it does break down barriers. Getting right with our partners, children, parents and friends starts with genuine regret followed by a heartfelt: 'I am *so* sorry!'

It would be too idealistic to think that people might always agree on every issue. We know that that is an impossibility. The problem arises in greater or smaller proportions, though, in ordinary families, in churches, in businesses – anywhere you find human beings.

The newspapers and radio and television journalists love it when there is a big political fall-out; they will latch on to an argument even to the point of exaggerating the positions. Such arguments are seen in policing policies, within the 'caring' professions, in the Fire Service – these are professions where a common purpose is paramount both in planning, and while working together. 'Standing on one's dignity' it is called because our natural position is not to concede an argument or point of view. We are right and the others are wrong. It's pride, isn't it? But this kind of attitude is easily broken if someone simply says 'sorry' and gets the response, 'Don't worry. I forgive you.' It's sad when people don't take that step. And I think it is especially sad when Christians hold on to unforgiveness, *especially* when Jesus prayed for us all to be 'one' – united in him (Jn. 13:34,35; 17:20–23).

Custard Christians

Do you know what 'a custard Christian' is? Someone who gets upset over trifles. Earlier, I mentioned my good friend and police colleague, Ron Perrett. Following that meeting he was addressing which erupted because some of the men couldn't or didn't recognise sin, Ron stayed on after everyone else had left and chatted with the secretary and treasurer of the mission. Ron remembered that because of the trouble, he had forgotten to tell the custard Christian joke, so he told it to them as they locked up. At least the evening ended with some mirth.

A week or so later, the secretary telephoned Ron and told him an amazing story. The secretary and treasurer had hardly spoken to each other for weeks because of a vehement disagreement. Despite Ron's talk, and the interruptions, God had used that time for his own purposes. For when Ron told the joke at the door *after* the meeting, the secretary and the treasurer were reminded of the triviality of their argument. They recognised that the joke was on them, stopped their laughter, both coincidently said 'sorry' and immediately sorted out their differences. Incredibly, the usual congregation at the mission knew of this argument and saw the healing which had taken place. Consequently, the work of the mission began to move forward again without any rancour.

And here is another story. A small church was struggling and all who attended knew exactly why. Two elderly members had had a conflict. The congregation divided their loyalties between them. This made any kind of progress impossible. They blatantly disregarded Jesus' instructions about forgiving others (see Mt. 6:14,15).

A new minister came to the church and spent several weeks teaching about forgiveness, trust and healing. He knew about the problem before he arrived and had spoken to each of the problem-makers individually without any tangible improvement. For some time, frustratingly for the minister, people in the church continued to stick to their divided loyalties and the feeling of distrust permeated all that was going on.

After much prayer, the minister felt compelled to take action. So during a morning service, and just before the sermon, he called both elderly men to come forward. Without any further explanation, he had them face each other and asked, in front of the congregation, each to openly forgive the other. He saw that this was a big risk and it could have caused havoc. He had been rather reticent to do this but nothing else had healed the breach which was ruining the worship and outreach of the church.

The pregnant pause didn't help. But gradually, one of the men made a move, and then the other, to the point where they were close enough to shake hands. The men had seen for themselves the pointlessness of their disagreement and audibly said 'sorry', asking for understanding and forgiveness. While they were hugging, the whole congregation stood with warm applause. The breach was healed. A very real breakthrough had occurred, evidenced by new people coming through the doors, the ministry beginning to bear fruit and the church becoming an outward looking-fellowship.[1]

The minister of the church when we lived in Surrey was invited to speak at a church anniversary service at another location. Frank Cooke was the celebrated and well-advertised visiting speaker. He had no idea about the congregation, its prayer life, its outreach and general standing in the community although he had heard that it was a lively evangelical fellowship. In his prayerful preparation, he was troubled that God seemed to have nothing for him to speak about! He had spoken at many similar services and could, had he chosen, used notes from previous engagements. But he rarely did that because he was disciplined enough to prepare *specifically*.

The day came but still he had nothing on paper and nothing special in mind – a complete blank! Very embarrassing for a visiting speaker; also rather nerve-wracking, as he admitted to me later.

Anyway, he arrived and was warmly welcomed. 'Looking forward to what you will have to say!' was the greeting.

The anniversary was well conducted and celebrated with great singing, prayer, Bible readings and members recalling days gone by when God had enriched and encouraged the church. Then Frank was announced with a flourish and great acclaim: 'We are so pleased to have such an accomplished speaker with us today.' As he leant over the pulpit very sheepishly, he simply said 'Thank you' and then he made his startling announcement: 'Friends, thank you for inviting me here but I have nothing to say to you!'

There was a huge intake of breath and a bit of murmuring. The congregation perhaps felt that the speaker was 'having them on'. One or two began to giggle and eventually a number started to laugh as he stood there – blankly.

'Seriously, in my preparation to come here it seemed as if God hasn't given me anything to say.'

There was still a feeling that this was part of the message, a funny start to a great address but gradually it dawned on the church that he really did have *nothing* to say.

'But he's the visiting speaker!' could be heard amid the murmuring.

After some minutes of a very awkward silence, an elderly gentleman gradually got to his feet, and as he stood in the midst of the congregation, he said, rather hesitatingly, 'I think I may be the cause of this embarrassment.' He trembled as he went on, 'Some weeks ago, I had a dreadful disagreement with one of the deacons about the continuous change which we have to tolerate in this church. It turned into a terrible argument as he stood up for the minister. I stood my ground but have now come to realise that I was in the wrong and I want to say sorry right now . . . to the deacon over there and to you all here today.' He sank to his seat and buried his face in his hands weeping loudly. As he did so, another man stood up; it was the deacon, on the other side of the church.

He called across to the first man, in a wavering voice, tears in his eyes. 'Thank you. I forgive you here and now. And I have to say that I was equally wrong in not properly listening to you. I am so sorry.'

The two men slowly left their seats and, meeting each other in an aisle, hugged and wept.

As they did so, Frank Cooke watched from the pulpit as a small but significant stirring began in the pews facing him. People began to move to speak to someone else; there was crying, there was laughter, there was forgiveness and sorrow. Much hugging, relief and joy . . . oh yes, God had spoken through the speaker's silence and the church had begun to move forward again. What an amazing experience where the speaker's silence spoke volumes.

One other thing about forgiveness here. Sometimes, Christians say they forgive, but there seem to be strings attached. '*If* you . . . *then* I will forgive.' We need to understand that forgiveness must be unconditional – and treat others as Jesus treats us.

Conclusion

Forgiveness is an important thing indeed; yes, seeking it from others is hard, but I believe it's crucial if we want to live free of bitterness and restriction.

Consider Jesus' words in Matthew's Gospel (6:14), well put in THE MESSAGE:

> In prayer there is a connection between what God does and what you do. You can't get forgiveness from God, for instance, without also forgiving others. If you refuse to do your part, you cut yourself off from God's part

Restoration with others is not only beautiful to behold, it sets us free.

Notes

[1] Source: *Our Daily Bread*, Radio Bible Class, PO Box 1, Carnforth, Lancashire, LA5 9ES. Used with permission.

4

Love for hate

If, after we have acknowledged our sin, come to Jesus, believing he is the answer, and sought restoration, how can we continue to live for him in an attitude of peace and forgiveness – even towards those who have wronged or continue to wrong us?

Renewed and reformed

There is absolutely no doubt that a life is truly renewed and reformed when two things happen (i) there is genuine repentance and (ii) a turning to Christ who will transform anyone believing in him by forgiveness, giving new life, a new beginning and strength to live his way. And of course, as I have mentioned before, this is not a sudden turning over of a new leaf, becoming religious, turning up at church more often, changing attitudes or even having a new identity.

I refer to a *relationship* with the living Jesus who by his Spirit lives in a person who truly and realistically repents of wrongdoing. This will be recognised by others as a change of life and character. And such a person will need the support and encouragement of others. That's where church fellowship is important – not just filling a pew on Sunday mornings but joining in the 'family' and being part of the worship, the teaching and the outreach of a local fellowship.

Change does not go unnoticed. One of the most poignant accounts in the Bible is the change that came over a man called Onesimus. We read his story in the book of Philemon. He was a runaway slave – a capital offence under Roman law – who, it is thought, stole from his master, Philemon. The slave eventually got to Rome where he somehow met Paul who was under house arrest there for his Christian belief. Paul evidently took time to show Onesimus the error of his ways and helped him to become a Christian. Paul must have seen that the best way of showing how the slave had changed was to send him back to Philemon – a tall order for Onesimus! But he went, clutching a letter from Paul which contained a plea to accept Onesimus back because of the complete change in his life even to the point that he might call him 'brother'. Such a simple petition which depicts all that I have tried to say about forgiveness here.

But that change has to happen within. Jesus promised the Spirit to anyone who follows him – he likened the new life bubbling up inside of us as 'a spring of water welling up to eternal life' (Jn. 4:13). This is the power we need to live for Christ. And this is the power we need to be able to forgive those who have sinned against us.

Love in return for love is quite natural; love in return for hate is supernatural! The fact is, though, we can be transformed. The Bible says that '. . . if anyone is in Christ, he is a new creation; the old has gone, the new has come!' (2 Cor. 5:17). That does not mean being religious, *trying* to be good or anything else that makes us feel better. It is a gift from God, who settled the relationship between us and him and then calls us to settle our relationships with each other. God put the world right with himself through Jesus, giving us the chance of a fresh start by offering forgiveness of sins. And God has given us the task of telling everyone what he is doing – we are ambassadors of Christ in the world (2. Cor. 5:20).

None of this talks about revenge or trying to get our own back. By accepting what God offers and then making the same offer to those who don't know him, we begin to live a different way. How? Through his power alone. Power *he gives us by his own life living in us*.

If we feel we simply *cannot* forgive, we must ask him to do it through us, and trust him to do just that. If we did, I feel there would be a huge change in society; think about the consequences in the home! I think that the divorce rate would begin to shrink, the separation of partners would be rare; children would see this great example of reconciliation and warmth and hopefully, follow the example – taking it into schools and ultimately into the world as they grow up.

Examples

I have had the privilege of meeting and spending time with Corrie Ten Boom and Pastor Richard Wurmbrandt. Their stories and others should be our inspiration to love our enemies.

Corrie was a teenage girl living with her sister and parents in Haarlem, Holland during World War Two. The Nazis overran the country and began their 'cleansing' so that all Jewish people were hunted down to be taken to concentration camps in Germany and Poland.

Corrie's home was used to hide Jews who were fleeing from their pursuers; my daughter Judi and her family used to live nearby and I have been to those very rooms above their watch and clockmaker's shop. A neighbour informed on them so that the Ten Boom family was violently arrested and transported away by rail in animal wagons. Corrie's parents didn't survive the journey but she and her sister, Betsy, were together in a lice-ridden, dank and dirty wooden hut which leaked in bad weather, had no heating and hardly any water for washing. There was very little food. They were at the mercy of lustful German soldiers and depraved SS officers . . . you can read about it in Corrie's book *The Hiding Place*.[1]

The point of this is that Corrie had every reason to hate the regime and its henchmen. Her parents were dead, and Betsy didn't survive pneumonia and malnutrition. But Corrie told me that at no time did she hate her captors, however cruelly she was treated. Corrie never was bitter because she prayed for the guards every day by name; she only despised *what they did*. God used her testimony in the years after the war ended as she spoke of Jesus' love; again, she never spoke a bitter word about the Nazis and SS – she said that she forgave them, and prayed again and again that they would become Christians.

Some years after the war, Corrie was speaking in Munich and after the church service, she saw a man she recognised as one of her guards – an SS man. She said the awful memories came flooding back and, although the former guard came to her and spoke of his being forgiven by God, she could not shake his hand. She still felt anger and although she preached forgiveness, this seemed an impossible moment. She silently prayed for forgiveness of her attitude, but it was *still* impossible for her to shake his hand. She prayed again. Somehow God got through to her and, as she took this man's hand, it was as if God's forgiveness flowed through her to him. She felt that when Jesus asks us to love our enemies, he somehow gives *his* love *through* us.

A Bible is in the lounge of Corrie's old home and is still open at the page the family was reading together when the SS raided. Romans Chapter 8 it was – 'we are more than conquerors through him who loved us' (v.37). Corrie herself said, 'You never so touch the ocean of God's love as when you forgive and love your enemies.'[2]

Richard Wurmbrandt was an evangelical pastor of a small church in Romania. The communists, while tolerating the Orthodox Church, condemned any other Christian form of worship. Richard stood for his faith but paid the penalty by arrests and several terms of imprisonment. Nothing would deter him from his faith and he was never broken. He was frequently kept naked in his cell, with no toilet facilities and of course, no Bible. The guards mocked him daily and reached their nadir by giving him a sham communion using his faeces and urine as bread and wine.

Richard, starved and ill, prayed daily for his sneering guards and was able to introduce one of them to the Christian faith. Then that guard was arrested and became a fellow prisoner, suffering the same degradation.

When I last met Richard just before his move to America, he said that he never doubted God, never wavered in his faith and always loved not only his guards but also the leaders of his beloved Romania. He told me that he forgave them daily and finally on his release, repeated Jesus' words '. . . they didn't know what they were doing.' And, of course, Jesus said, 'Love your enemies . . .'

Another example of amazing forgiveness can be found in Craig Nelson's book, *The First Heroes*. This recounts how the Doolittle Raiders launched their first major counter-attack on the Pacific front during World War Two. Not all the raiders returned from their bombing mission. Jacob DeShazer was among those who were captured and held in Japanese prisoner of war camps under harsh and painful circumstances of depravity and humiliation. After the war, DeShazer returned to Japan but not to seek revenge; he had received Jesus as his Saviour and gone back to Japanese soil carrying the message of Christ. A former warrior who was once on a campaign of war was now on a campaign of reconciliation.[3]

DeShazer's mission to Japan mirrors the heart of the Saviour who himself came on a mission of love and reconciliation. When Christ came into the world, it was not merely to be a moral example or a compelling teacher. He came to look for and to save the lost. His love for us found its expression in the cross, and his rescue of the world found its realisation when he emerged triumphantly from the tomb in resurrected life. Job done; the sacrifice accepted by his heavenly Father.

These modern 'saints' followed their Saviour's example. In their stories we also find another clue about how it is possible to love our enemies . . . we have to pray for them! Is that so difficult? Well, yes it is and therefore part of that prayer must be to ask for God's own love. Again, it is his power not ours that will enable us to forgive.

Turning it round

Let these words of the apostle Paul really sink into your mind and heart:

> Bless your enemies; no cursing under your breath. Laugh with your happy friends when they're happy; share tears when they're down. Get along with each other; don't be stuck-up. Make friends with the nobodies; don't be the great somebody.

Don't hit back; discover beauty in everyone. If you've got it in you, get along with everybody. Don't insist on getting even; that's not for you to do. 'I'll do the judging,' says God, 'I'll take care of it.'

Our Scriptures tell us that if you see your enemy hungry, go buy that person lunch; or if thirsty, give him a drink. Your generosity will surprise him with goodness. Don't let evil get the best of you; get the best of evil by doing good' (Rom. 12:14–21).

Or as someone once said, turn *evil* round and *live*! Get it?

But with all that in mind, even if it were learnt off by heart, nothing would happen unless our inner attitude is changed. Turning hate into love is something only God can do.

We hear of wars and rumours of war and every day the national News brings the ravages of worldwide conflict into the living room. It appears that commentators recognise that humanity looks to *force* as a first resort instead of opening a door to negotiate and listen to another point of view, and hopefully look to conciliation.

Tension between nations, disputes about borders, arguments about arms control . . . which of these lead to peaceful existence? Have the concepts of apology and forgiveness left the negotiating table? Have they been extensively explored? I would suggest that such attitudes are very rare.

Conclusion

In Christ we find forgiveness and that forgiveness changes our life and our eternity – all because he came on a campaign of reconciliation. He loved us and gave himself for us. When we come to Christ, we must take the lead from Jesus, take courage and strength from him and make a real difference in our world so that it might flow out from home, to street, to village and town, to country and even the world. Do you believe that too idealistic? If so, I urge you to stop for a moment and reflect upon the examples above. Turning evil around – love for hate . . . true stories, true love.

Notes

[1] Corrie Ten Boom with John and Elizabeth Sherrill, *The Hiding Place* (London: Hodder & Stoughton, 1991).
[2] Quoted in John Blanchard's *Gathered Gold* (Welwyn, Herts: Evangelical Press, 1984).
[3] Quoted from *Our Daily Bread*, Radio Bible Class, PO Box 1, Carnforth, Lancashire, LA5 9ES. Used with permission.

5

Getting it wrong

I think I have made it quite clear that even after we give our lives to Christ, it will not be easy to live wholeheartedly for him all the time.

Do you remember the built-in bias we talked about earlier? We have to realise that the bias may affect our life unless we give complete control to the Master into whose hands we have committed our life.

On that first day for me on the bowling green playing the sport which is described as non-physical, I had the painful experience of a wood from another rink clattering into my fingers as I bent to pick up my own wood. I was the novice but it taught me that even the experts can get it wrong; that wood had been rolled by someone who knew about the game but he took too little care about where the bias would take his wood. We have to be careful to 'crucify' our flesh on a daily basis – that means, making a conscious effort to obey God's leading in thought and deed. Yes, he will give us power to live for him – but we must want to!

I know just how much I have had to be forgiven; it is an immense amount. The sin with which I was born has had to be dealt with as also the failings which I have had to constantly confess; thank God that I can say again and again 'I keep a grip on hope; God's loyal love couldn't have run out; his merciful love couldn't have dried up. They're created new every morning. How great is his faithfulness. I'm sticking with God!' (Lam. 3:21–24, THE MESSAGE).

We may have decided we're 'sticking with God' and want Jesus to be Number One in our lives – we're no longer pew-sitters saying 'Let's not go overboard. We mustn't take it too far!' for we have not forgotten or ignored the fact that Jesus went all the way to Calvary for us. How dare we, any of us, fail to forgive others when the forgiveness that we can receive from God cost him so much? He, in his love for the whole world, gave his Son for us. But we need to live for him in reality – daily.

Check your status

When we do fail him and get it wrong, and we surely will, for we aren't perfect, there is no need to go around being miserable.

I am reminded of an incident when our young people at Purley were out on the streets and attempting to witness. They asked a middle-aged, well-dressed man if he would mind answering a few questions.

He asked, 'Is this about God and your church up the road?'

'Yes,' they said.

'Well, no thanks,' said the man, 'I've enough troubles now without adding to them and making myself even more miserable!'

What a perception. Is that how Christians are seen? Really, that's not what Christians should be like, is it? It isn't how we should be perceived. Jesus promised us life in abundance; he turned water into wine, not the other way round. He brings joy!

In Revelation 3:1–6, the risen and glorified Lord Jesus described the church at Sardis, and I believe it reflects many of today's churches of whatever denomination. We hear today of churches where God is not actually at the centre of things, don't we? Arguments about whether to have pews or not, who is doing the flowers and where should they be placed, how the minister dresses, whether women be involved in ministry, what time we should have the services, should we still have evening worship? And so on. We debate the kind of communion we should celebrate; should we have just an organ or are other instruments permitted? Then there are the weekly decisions as to where we should sit. What do we do about newcomers who come in? Should we get up and welcome them or simply ignore them?

Surely the real priority is to be right with God and ensure that that relationship reflects the Lord Jesus, who welcomed everyone in rich, warm and humble humanity. 'Think of yourselves the way Christ thought of himself. He had equal status with God but didn't think so much of himself that he had to cling to the advantages of that status no matter what' (Phil. 2:6, THE MESSAGE).

Here's an interesting story about status and forgiveness. One day, Jesus was invited to dinner by a religious man, a Pharisee named Simon. Simon could be likened to many today who are respectable people, perhaps church-goers – pillars of society.

It seems that Jesus did not receive even a polite welcome which would normally be expected at that time in the Middle East. While he was there, a woman came to the house and poured perfume on Jesus' feet, wiping them with her hair. This prompted Simon to say to himself, 'If Jesus was really a prophet, he'd know what sort of woman she is. She's a prostitute.'

'Simon,' said Jesus, 'I've got something to tell you.' And he told the Pharisee the story of two men who were in debt to a money-lender. One owed ten times more than the other but neither had sufficient money to pay up. So the money-lender cancelled both debts.

Jesus asked Simon, 'Which of these two men do you think will be more grateful?'

Simon replied, 'I suppose the one who owed the most.'

'Yes,' said Jesus, 'You're right.' He went on to point out that Simon had offered him none of the usual courtesies, but that the woman had shown how much she loved him because of what she had done for him.

> 'Therefore, I tell you, her many sins have been forgiven – for she loved much. But he who has been forgiven little loves little.' Then Jesus said to her, 'Your sins are forgiven' (Lk. 7:47,48).

Simon had got it wrong. The woman had got it right. Don't let religious attitudes get in the way of your walk with Jesus.

Yes, we'll get it wrong at times. We'll take our eyes off Jesus; without knowing it, our love will grow cold and our churches will feel dead. There are going to be times, and many of them, when we will want our own way, not his. But look at this reassuring promise:

> If my people, who are called by my name, will humble themselves and pray and seek my face and turn from their wicked ways, then will I hear from heaven and will forgive their sin and will heal their land (2 Chron. 7:14).

We note the conditions here – God's people need to humble themselves in order for God to forgive. (If only we would really do this – bow the head, admit the sin, pray and repent, deliberately turning away from it . . . look, he promises to heal our land!) Ask, and he will forgive. Yes, he will forgive us whatever we have done, whatever we have been in the habit of doing, whatever we have *not* done . . . God sees through the veneer which covers our real life, the façade of being what we are not. Be assured, we cannot fool him by going through the motions of a Christian lifestyle without a heart commitment to him.

A lesson from King David

Thinking about being forgiven after getting it very wrong, I remembered King David in the Old Testament. He saw the naked Bathsheba having a bath and in his lust, committed adultery with her. Worse was to come; Bathsheba became pregnant, so David tried all manner of deceit to hide what he had done. In the end, he had Bathsheba's soldier husband sent to the very heart of the battle where, as David had anticipated and hoped, he was killed in the line of duty never knowing about his wife's disloyalty with the king (see 2 Sam. 11).

Later, as would be expected, there was deep remorse that he had fallen so low. In his depression, he just had to get right with his God; so he confessed his sin as we read in Psalm 51: 'Against you, you only have I sinned and done what is evil in your sight . . . Create in me a clean heart, O God . . . Restore to me the joy of your salvation (vv. 4.10,12).

Maybe our sin is not in the category of David's, though in reality in thought and intent it may well be as bad. Jesus said even the thought was as bad as the action (see Mt. 5:27,28) so clearly, no sin is small in God's eyes. And that's what makes forgiveness for all, even the worst of us, possible; we've *all* missed the mark, we're *all* in the same boat and Christ is the *only* way to God for any of us.

Do we need to humble ourselves to pray like David, so that God can thoroughly cleanse and renew us as he forgives all our sin? David recorded his experience with God in Psalm 103. Take time to read it. It will bless your soul.

The continuing and never diluted message yells at us all to 'seek the LORD while he may be found; call on him while he is near. Let the wicked forsake his way and the evil man his thoughts. Let him turn to the LORD, and he will have mercy on him . . .' (Is. 55:6,7).

Conclusion

I have a quiet time each morning at the beginning of the day. I have in front of me at the desk these words, based on Jeremiah's words in Lamentations chapter 3: 'I call this to mind and therefore have hope – because of the Lord's love I am not overcome and because his compassion never comes to an end. To me they are renewed every morning – I say "Lord, great is your faithfulness" and that's why I hope in him.'

So, if you're struggling, don't despair. Remember, David fell and fell hard. But God had called him 'a man after his own heart' (1 Sam. 13:14). Great is our Lord's faithfulness. Hope in him.

6

Living it

My wife and I have lived in our present home for twenty years or so. We have had some lovely neighbours and we all look out for each other to help whenever needed and also we frequently meet in each other's homes. Our original next door neighbours died within months of each other and following the sale of their bungalow, the new incumbents immediately began planning for an extension and vast alterations so that builders were there for another twelve months before the home was reoccupied. Sadly, the extension completely obliterated our view of the sea, which had been one of the reasons we bought our house. However, losing a view is not a valid objection to Planning Authorities.

Our new neighbours asked us about the improvements which, in themselves are fine. But we mentioned the view – or lack of it. It was not said acrimoniously; life is too precious to have that sort of argument. Having mentioned it, our neighbour said that he hadn't thought of that and apologised profusely.

'Please, it's not an issue,' we said, 'you're forgiven anyway!' And we meant it. But the fact is, life is full of these little (and not so little) irritants that can so easily escalate. We *don't* always feel like forgiving. We can bottle it up and before we know it, we're in the grip of bitter unforgiveness.

I found as a chief officer of police, when considering personnel for promotion or a specialist post that long memories came into play. Firstly, the officer may remember something done years before and, although it was dealt with, can't stop asking: 'Will it count against me?' Secondly, senior colleagues who continually call to mind the incident, mistake or error of judgement. It's not too difficult to get alongside the officer and be reassuring that the past is gone. But listening to much-respected colleagues who are allowing their memory to cloud their mind in respect of how an officer performs *here and now* is a different matter. I suspect that the police service is not alone in keeping long memories and many are the employees who have suffered for it.

Time and again, I have asked about a particular officer – a constable or sergeant – who, in my view, had shown good qualities. But I would hear: 'No, sir, not suitable. Some years ago he made a dreadful misjudgement and your predecessor had to fine him two days' pay.' Or: 'Sir, you won't remember, but she failed to fill in her Report Book in the case of an accident.'

But what about now? That's past and gone, surely.

'Has the lesson been learnt?' I'd ask.

That to me was far more important than an historical incident. Long memories like that are totally out of place unless, of course, there hasn't been a change. In which case, what are the supervising officers doing about it?

This is the scriptural principle of community living – in village or town, at work, in sport and leisure. Listen to Jesus' words:

Don't pick on people, jump on their failures, criticize their faults – unless, of course, you want the same treatment.

Don't condemn those who are down; that hardness can boomerang. Be easy on people; you'll find life a lot easier. Give away your life; you'll find life given back, but not merely given back – given back with bonus and blessing. Giving, not getting, is the way. Generosity begets generosity (Lk. 6:36,37, THE MESSAGE).

And the more challenging words, just before that:

Love your enemies. Let them bring out the best in you, not the worst. When someone gives you a hard time, respond with the energies of prayer for that person. If someone slaps you in the face, stand there and take it. If someone grabs your shirt, giftwrap your best coat and make a present of it. If someone takes unfair advantage of you, use the occasion to practice the servant life. No more tit-for-tat stuff. Live generously' (Lk. 6:27-31, THE MESSAGE).

I have actually heard a high court judge say to acrimonious parties in front of him and to combating lawyers: 'Can you all please cease this bickering and listen for one moment?' Listen to each other and recognise that forgiveness with compassion is perhaps the greatest gift we could all possess. Why don't you all learn that lesson here in Court today?' That brought a stunned silence!

What the judge said is an undeniable truth but it takes tremendous courage to swallow pride, look another in the eye and say 'I'm sorry' or 'I forgive you.'

From the heart

Jesus once told a story about debtors. A king had a servant who owed him a great deal of money. He wasn't able to pay the debt so the king ordered that he and his wife and children and all that he had be sold to repay the debt. The man begged for mercy and the king cancelled the debt. Then the man found one of his fellow-servants, someone who owed him a paltry sum, and demanded, with violence, to be paid in full. He refused this fellow-servant any kind of mercy. When the king heard of this, he immediately rescinded his favour and had the unmerciful servant thrown into prison (see Mt. 18:23–35). *That*, said Jesus, was how our heavenly Father will treat us if we don't forgive from the heart.

The first character, though he was freed of a heavy debt, didn't really appreciate what forgiveness was; hence his own diabolical behaviour towards his former friend. The message is clear: 'Do to others as you would have them do to you.'

Jesus told this story soon after he had answered Peter's question, 'Lord, how many times shall I forgive my brother when he sins against me? Up to seven times?' Jesus replied, 'I tell you, not seven times but seventy-seven times' – that is, times without number (see Mt. 18:21,22).

Note the emphasis of Jesus 'forgive from the heart'. Saying that we forgive unless we are sincere is meaningless. Mere words, especially grudging words, are simply not good enough. It is nowhere near the mark just thinking that we *ought* to forgive because that's what the Good Book says or that maybe it would impress others and make a show of being helpful, merciful and forgiving. That's a sham. Our attitude is what is so important and at the core of forgiveness. We need to actually mean what we say, genuinely forgive and then perhaps add the icing to the cake, invite that person to the house, or go out for coffee together and so on. That's what really makes things right. OK, it isn't easy; we may not want to. But we *can* do it, in Christ.

Having said that, in my experience it is much easier to accuse than to forgive; so, forgiveness is a very difficult path to tread. Paul sums it up perfectly by revealing what God had said to him, 'My grace is sufficient for you, for my power is made perfect in weakness' (2 Cor. 12:9).

Whether we find forgiveness easy or difficult, we have to have the attitude which *wants* to forgive and go through with it whatever the cost. This is the attitude of Christ. Personally, I cannot believe that forgiveness of anyone is an easy option whoever they are, strangers or friends. While I know how much I have appreciated being forgiven by parents, sisters, my wife, my children and others, that's what really drives me to seek to forgive others. But I still have to steel myself and ask the question, 'What is my motive here?'

Having said that, reaction to forgiveness does not always bring rapturous applause. I call to mind one of the most publicised statements of forgiveness, by the late President Gerald Ford in the United States of America. He came to office when as Vice President his boss President Richard Nixon had been accused of orchestrating the notorious Watergate scandal for which many of his senior aides were found guilty and served terms of imprisonment. As a result, Nixon was impeached and driven from office. But sometime later, Gerald Ford openly forgave him as a personal gesture. Perhaps this unpopular decision was also soured because Gerald Ford overruled justice and also formally pardoned Nixon instead of insisting that he faced the Courts for crimes against the people.

Forgiveness should never dilute or interfere with the justice system in any country and I quote that example to underline that principle. At the other end of the scale, maybe in a driving scenario, I suppose it is possible to feel sorry for another driver who has lost control of their vehicle because of excessive speed and collided with your front wall. We could well do the same. We might be able to forgive the driver but that should not interfere with a police officer doing his duty in reporting the incident nor should it exonerate the driver from paying for the repairs or even answering a summons for excessive speed or driving without due care. Putting forgiveness into practice then is complex. But whatever the circumstances, don't put it off.

Memories

I have already touched on the effect that non-forgiveness has on our health and attitude. Frankly, whatever you do not forgive, you relive. That causes you to keep striking out at others and robs you of the joy of loving and being loved in return. What a loss! Non-forgiveness is an umbilical cord that keeps you tied to the past. Forgiveness allows you to cut that cord. When we refuse to forgive someone, we remain chained to memories that will continually affect us in a negative way.

In World War II, following the German invasion of France, a number of French people, presumably in fear for their families or their jobs, maybe even their lives, colluded with the Nazis. Many became informants about the Resistance movements, about Jewish citizens living in local towns and villages and about people who were known to be hiding servicemen wanted by the Gestapo. Naturally these collaborators were despised by most French people and it is said that after the war had ended, many of them were summarily dealt with, even by

hanging in the street, as a retribution for their betrayals
and crime. One might say, 'Serves them right' but, having satisfied themselves that justice had finally been
done, it was discovered that many of those who had
been punished had in fact been severely tortured by the
Nazis into revealing information and thus were not
really to blame. Such collaboration, if it can be called
that, was under extreme pain and pressure and subsequent ostracism and punishment was certainly not justi-
fied. Those who took retribution and had no thought of
forgiveness, lived to regret the day; many became ill
with guilt and shame and ended their days in mental
hospitals; their pall of depression left an inheritance of
bitterness, regret and bewilderment for their families.

Revenge and retaliation

If we don't forgive, we get involved in the very opposite – revenge and retaliation. We harbour hatred, bitterness and anger, most of which only hurt *us*. At the
very worst end of the scale, for instance in inner-city
ganglands, retribution often escalates and so we see
serious injury and even killings. Hatred breeds more
retaliation and hatred and so the downward spiral con-
tinues. Sometimes there are feuds which others have
inherited and no one can remember the cause. What is
it that makes us want to return injury and insult? Why
can't we take it like a sponge, then squeeze it out by
offering an olive branch of forgiveness? Perhaps the
running street battles and violent clashes we see on our
TV screens both in the UK and elsewhere are not our
personal scene. But at root, we have the same potential.
Let us cry out then, 'Heal me, O LORD, and I shall be
healed' (Jer. 17:14).

My early days of employment were in the Prison Commission and although I worked in Headquarters, I spent some time in prisons and borstals in England. Many of the men, women and young people – some convicted and some on remand awaiting trial – survived each day in fear and trembling, reluctant to leave their cell or dormitory, because of the bullies who unofficially 'ran' the place. The bullies called the shots!

There's little room for forgiving and forgetting in prison. Jonathan Aitken, the former MP who was incarcerated following a white-collar crime but became a Christian before he was found guilty and sentenced to a term of imprisonment, saw this kind of behaviour first-hand. He found that with the grace of God, who had forgiven him, he was able to lie low for a time. But eventually he had to come to terms with fellow inmates and was able to forgive those who taunted him. He was then accepted by some who needed him to write letters for them and read the replies. It is true to say that those who have been forgiven have so much to give to others – if we have been forgiven much, we will love much, as we have already seen in Luke 7:6–50.

I could use further examples from my working life to show you revenge and retaliation which starts in the heart and mind. However, that saddens me and I still wonder how, outside of new life in Christ, it is *ever* truly possible to deal with colossal hurts which would naturally mean taking revenge. Is it really possible to truly forgive from the heart in these situations, without his help? God's Holy Spirit is available to us who believe and provides a very real way of escape from that vengeful attitude. Part of the fruit of the Spirit, the result of the living God working in our lives, is self-control. In other words, there is much greater strength available than we can muster to deal with our natural inclination towards retaliation.

Christians really need to recognise that:

> No test or temptation that comes [our] way is beyond the course of what others have had to face. All [we] have to remember is that God will never let [us] down; he'll never let [us] be pushed past [our] limit; he'll always be there to help [us] come through it (1 Cor. 10:13, THE MESSAGE).

None of us is unique. We cannot legitimately plead that because of our lack of education, because of our upbringing or whatever excuse – many of which I have heard in a charge-room or before a magistrate – is what made us different and therefore more vulnerable to fall under temptation. But the Lord *promises* his followers that their temptations are not more than we will be able to bear and the way out is in the strength God supplies.

Only when we understand this and put it into practice can there be an example for others to follow. But we have to be in the grip of God for it to make any difference.

The Bible also tells us that part of the fruit of the Spirit is love (Gal. 5:22,23). It doesn't need a theologian to explain that. Evidently is it not talking about marital love or merely some emotional feeling. But to *love your enemy*? That's surely impossible in our own strength. It is not even possible to respect our enemies or tolerate them at a distance. Love them? How? Well, if Jesus commands it, there must be a way and that way is to be found in him and the power he gives. It is a fact that he does give that almost impossible ability if only we look to him for the resolve to do it. The fruit of the Spirit, as well as being self-control, is peace, patience, kindness and gentleness. All of these things and more are *the result* of Christ living in us. They are a gift from God. If we surrender to him, we will see this fruit being grown more and more in our lives, and any thoughts of anger, retaliation, of hardness towards others, should disappear or at least be under God's control.

That, simply, is how to 'live it'.

An example of loving enemies

I have had many battles with sworn enemies of police and had threats to my family and me from villains. This means that I have had really difficult challenges to my faith within this context of loving my enemy. But I am encouraged and challenged by others who have found God can do it where we can't. Consider this supreme example of 'loving your enemy'.

In the mid 1950s, an intrepid quintet of young men – Jim Elliot, Pete Fleming, Ed McCully and Roger Youderian together with their Missionary Aviation Fellowship pilot, Nate Saint – had an improbable ambition to reach the Auca Indians who lived in the Ecuador jungle, way up west in South America near one of the sources of the River Amazon.

The Auca tribe was virtually unknown by the civilised world and vice versa – the Indians had probably never seen the face of a white man. Rumours abounded in the jungle about their hostility so other jungle dwellers kept their distance. Nevertheless, these young men in their twenties were desperately keen to reach the unreached and to share with them the love of the Lord Jesus. They initially thought the response from the Aucas was welcoming, but how wrong they were. What happened is beyond imagination as one by one the five were unmercifully slaughtered by the Aucas. Sometime later, their bodies were discovered. You would think that that would have been the end of any further attempt to reach this vicious tribe. But years later, one of the men's widows summoned up courage to contact the other four wives with the intention of suggesting another attempt to reach the Aucas. No one would have blamed them if they'd condemned this tribe for ever, but no! Despite the loss of their husbands, they still wanted the Indians to hear of Jesus' love. These women eventually re-established contact with the tribe, all because they had in their hearts forgiven those who murdered their men.

Incredibly, the Aucas had changed and had become friendly. God had used the tragic deaths of those five young men to reach this godless tribe. Miracle of miracles, one of the killers was the first man converted and baptised. The love of these widows for a tribe, which in other circumstances, would have been their enemies for life enabled them to go back to make contact and then to live amongst them and introduce them to the good news of the gospel. What a remarkable account of 'loving your enemy'![1]

Conclusion

I hope it has become clear to you that Jesus would never have instructed us to do the impossible if he did not intend to give us the strength to overcome. In short, he never asks us to do what he won't give us the ability to do – if we look to him, rely on him and trust him. I think our biggest problem, when we have unforgiveness in our lives, is that most of us just can't bring ourselves to *want* to forgive – especially an enemy.

May I suggest that if you find this a really difficult concept to firstly consider who you think are your enemies? What is an enemy? Someone you don't like? Someone of whom you are jealous? A burglar or thief? Someone who has hurt you, wronged you? Hurt or wronged a loved one? Just *who* is your enemy? Is it at local level or bigger than that, even in an international sense? Here is a radical thought. Take specific time to pray for them, by name if you know them or in general if that's not feasible. I pray every day for the young man who was found guilty of killing our son; he is forgiven. I pray for him and his conscience, for his understanding of the grief he has caused to Lesley and her family, to my two daughters and to my wife and me. I'm praying that he may hear of and respond to the love of the Lord Jesus who can, incredibly, recreate his life while in prison. Nothing is impossible with God (Lk. 1:37).

Notes

[1] See Elisabeth Elliot *Through Gates of Splendour*, Copyright © 1956, 1957 The Auca Missionary Foundation (Milton Keynes: Authentic Media, 2006); and Elisabeth Elliot *Shadow of the Almighty* (Milton Keynes: Authentic Media, 2005).

Transitions

There was once a murderous man called Saul.

Had he been alive today his religious fanaticism might well have made him into a terrorist, in that he was prepared to pursue Christians to prison and even death for their beliefs. In his time – 2,000 years ago – he was regarded as a respected member of the Jewish community, bent on upholding their ancestral beliefs. He was known and feared by Christians throughout Israel. He was behind the murder of the first martyr, Stephen – 'Saul was there, giving approval to his death' (Acts 8:1) and we read on that 'Saul just went wild, devastating the church, entering house after house after house, dragging men and women off to jail' (THE MESSAGE). In police terms, Saul was at least an accessory but probably the leader behind the planning of the incursions.

Notorious

So notorious was he that the church was in deep dread of what would come next; followers of Christ were scattered out of Jerusalem to Judea and Samaria and even further. The account shows that 'Saul was still breathing out murderous threats against the Lord's disciples. He went to the high priest and asked him for letters to the synagogues in Damascus, so that if he found any there who belonged to the Way, whether men or women, he might take them as prisoners to Jerusalem' (Acts 9:1,2). Saul even had the high priest and all the hierarchy in the Jewish faith of the day on his side in this dramatic and terrifying persecution.

Yet, in a miraculous and absolutely amazing way, God was able to completely transform this one-time zealot into one of the great saints in the history of the Christian Church. It reminds me of a newspaper editor who had learned that a man named Alfred Nobel had died and he assumed without checking that the deceased must be the same man who invented dynamite. So he published an obituary calling Nobel 'the merchant of death'. But when the real Alfred Nobel read the account of his 'own' death, he reacted like a blind man suddenly gaining sight. From that startling day for him, Nobel devoted himself to philanthropic causes, especially peace and most of us have recognised his transformation by reading of the Nobel Peace Prize winners.[1]

Saul of Tarsus experienced a transformation far more dramatic than Alfred Nobel's. While on the road to Damascus with his evil intent, God met him in an extraordinary way – he heard the voice of the risen Lord Jesus. Saul was temporarily blind after this experience and had to be led to Damascus, not now the fanatic looking for victims but a man being changed by God. There is no other explanation. True for Saul and the world to discover that God doesn't want anyone to be lost – 'He's giving everyone space and time to change' (2 Pet. 3:9, THE MESSAGE).

Saul *was* transformed; it was an earth-shattering experience for him to change from terrorising Jesus' disciples to becoming a disciple himself. But the fact is, God was able to forgive this man. But what about the transition? Could those who had been hunted down by Saul, those who cowered in his presence, those who knew of his murderous acts, ever accept him as a friend and embrace him now as one who was genuinely converted? The change was not simply that Saul, whose name was now changed to Paul, had ceased to persecute Christians. He wanted to worship with them. He was, in our modern terms, going to church, slipping into a pew and joining in with church activities!

Saul or Paul had literally begun living again. Life, for a man who was maybe in his thirties, had started again from scratch despite the fact that he was mature and well-educated. This was no resolution, it was a human *revolution*. I often hear some people pooh-poohing the phrase 'born again' and it is so easy to snipe at something which seems like 'taking religion too far' but who could deny that this happened in Paul's life? I reckon it is very foolish – even dangerous – to jeer at and criticise such an experience.

The ultimate question in Paul's experience was – how would Christians react to his conversion? We understand that their fear took time to dispel (e.g. see Acts 9:13) but how can we blame them? How incredible it was that Ananias, who'd been scared of this man, went to see Paul and immediately called him 'brother'. Paul lost his blindness and as a new Christian, he was very soon baptised, giving a public declaration of his new-found faith.

Nevertheless, some of the Christians were still murmuring about Paul especially once they heard him preach. Those who heard him asked the same question, 'Isn't he the man who caused havoc in Jerusalem among those who call on [Jesus]? And hasn't he come here to take them as prisoners to the chief priests?' (Acts 9:21).

This was a genuine and complete change in Paul's life, so much so that the very people on whose behalf he had been persecuting were now conspiring to kill *him*! He escaped their clutches and went to Jerusalem but when he tried to join the disciples there they were afraid, not believing that he was a transformed man. They naturally thought Paul was a 'plant' – an agent in disguise identifying any who might be part of the new Christian church (Acts 9:26). It took time for him to be accepted and it was finally the bravery of Barnabas, who later became a real companion and encourager of Paul, to speak up on his behalf and give powerful testimony of Paul's conversion on the way to Damascus. An enemy changed; an enemy loved!

Ultimately Christian believers recognised what God had done and were able to forgive Paul his terrifying persecutions and fanaticism. What a transformation! The point here is two-fold. No one is beyond being forgiven and changed by God. And we should forgive for who are we to withhold forgiveness from those God has forgiven? Haven't we been forgiven ourselves? Even if the person we must forgive doesn't know God and may not repent of their actions, we must let it go and pray for them. Who knows – like Saul, they may experience a sudden and amazing transition on their own road to Damascus. God can change anyone. Please don't turn your back on those who *need* your forgiveness. Believe in that transition to come.

Hurt by loved ones

But what about people we know well who have hurt us? Do we still need convincing that they should be forgiven too?

Here is a story from the book of Genesis in the Old Testament. How would you feel if you had brothers who were jealous of you because of your intellect, your abilities and your ambition? Jealous to the point of feigning your death and selling you off as a slave to another country? Well, that's what happened to a young man called Joseph. As a result he lived away from his parents and family for many years, suffering the indignity of false imprisonment before succeeding in the Egyptian Civil Service.

A considerable time later, Joseph met with his brothers again on a chance encounter when, with famine in their own country, the brothers came to Egypt to seek food enough to take home to their father, Jacob. The Lloyd-Webber/Rice musical *Joseph and the Amazing Technicolour Dreamcoat* is a wonderful portrayal of this incredible saga. The final scenario in this drama brought Joseph's father to Egypt – he thought Joseph was dead. It was such an emotional scene as they embraced and as Joseph forgave his brothers for their incomprehensible deception. Joseph was able to welcome his long-lost family and supply all their needs. With his gracious attitude simply he said that while they meant all they did for evil, God was able to turn it for good (Gen. 50:20). Joseph was in a position to ignore their pleas for help but he loved them, he forgave them and they were once again a reunited family.

Now if a man can have such a generous attitude towards his contemptible brothers, surely this is an example from which to learn. Can't forgive a family member? Remember Joseph and how God promises to bring about good from bad in the lives of those who love him (Rom. 8:28).

I feel sad when I think of families that have gone for months and even years with no hint of forgiveness; never even thinking about trying to hold out a hand of love and friendship. Then come the funerals but sometimes even death cannot heal the differences.

Experience tells me that when someone is forgiven, they will more often than not recognise their wrong and try to put it right. Sometimes it takes time but it's worth waiting for. Yes, there may be a period of doubt; a suspicion that repentance isn't genuine or sincere but when it dawns that the new attitude is real – that's when there can be peace and healing on both sides.

Willie Mullan

We have looked at Saul/Paul, but a much more up-to-date example of transition and change is Willie Mullan. He was a ne'er-do-well in Northern Ireland; a smelly, unwashed and alcoholic teenager. He had given up school and what home comforts he had had in his poverty-stricken family. He slept rough or, if he could steal a bed, in a hostel. Willie was not a man who could be loved. He was always in the wrong company and while he was not agile or intelligent enough to break into houses, he had his use as a lookout while the burglars were ransacking and thieving. His laziness and lethargy also gave him the job of 'casing the joint' from a hiding place in fields, behind hedges and so on, while a burglary was being planned. His expertise, if you could call it that, was to note when householders and children were out shopping, at work, at school or note the times when they came home and so on. He would watch for coffee mornings and other visits like the paper-boy, the milkman, etc. and then feed back the information for a pittance. (Please, I am not giving lessons!)

It was while Willie Mullan was lying in a field in long grass adjoining a grand house that a children's hymn came into his mind. He had apparently been dragged to an evangelistic mission where the preacher had banged on about God's wrath, which in turn sparked memories of his Sunday school days. It was enough to trigger a deep remorse about his drinking, his thieving, his dishonesty, his wasted life . . . This was sufficient for him to try and pray and to start thinking about finding God. He began to plead with God to meet with him, to change his life.

Willie left the field and the watching of the house only to be beaten up by his so-called friends. But rather than go back to his usual haunts, he sought accommodation elsewhere – though this usually failed because he was so unkempt, filthy and just not wanted.

But Christ wanted him. Jesus completely changed Willie Mullan. God met with him and forgave him. Very sadly, local Christian folk didn't want to know. He tried going to church while still unwashed, unshaven and dishevelled but was barred time and again by stewards who turned him away. He had the same reaction everywhere he went – word had got round as to who he was and maybe people thought he would be preying on them – but one Sunday evening, at what looked like a community centre rather than a church, he saw people going in and arrived at the door to join them. In fact, it was a Brethren Assembly and their evening gospel service. He was invited in and even though he was ushered to a back seat he felt there was hope at last. One man did go to speak with him and welcome him even to the point of sitting with him. From that one service, comfortable accommodation was found for him. He could at last wash and get his clothes cleaned. Later he was given second-hand clothing too. What he did for money was not clear but he was eventually given a part-time job.

People who like to be known as Christians had turned Willie away; no chance of acceptance or forgiveness there. He felt himself to be so unwanted and it must have been really tempting to give up – except that he had had an encounter with God. He was eventually welcomed, otherwise the world would never have known the powerful testimony and preaching – and the sympathetic pastoral gifts – of Willie Mullan. What a transition![2]

Conclusion

As we think about the change in someone like Saul, and in Willie Mullan, we can see that forgiveness by God transforms our lives. Forgiving others will transform it too. No one is beyond God's reach. *Anyone*, even the person who has hurt us most, can undergo a transition when they have met with God. So we need to pray for them. Can you do that? Or are you still nursing your hurt – 'You don't know what they did to me.' Like Joseph, we can see God working out *everything* for our good, so that we may even get to bless those who have hurt us. Let's be encouraged to put everything into his hands – our whole lives – and trust him for the good, even when we cannot see how that might occur; I don't suppose Joseph saw the good when he was in a foreign prison. But things worked out well in the end, for God was in control all the time.

I think we all need to thoroughly examine ourselves and be honest about our attitude to forgiveness. Do we say 'I forgive' and yet still resent what was said and despise the person who said it? Are we holding a grudge against anyone? Maybe we have said 'I can forgive but I can never forget'. Ask God to help you forget like he deliberately forgets *our* sin. And move on.

Maybe, as we come to the end of this book, we can see an opportunity for us to drop our guard and search our hearts. Then we can be liberated by unloading those burdens. Forgive and you will be forgiven; do it. How? With Christ's help. He can even give you the desire to do it – if you ask him.

Notes

1. Quoted from *Our Daily Bread*, Radio Bible Class, P.O. Box 1, Carnforth, Lancashire, LA5 9ES. Used with permission.
2. You can read Willie Mullan's story as told to Gladys and Derrick Knowlton in *Tramp After God* (Lakeland: Marshall, Morgan & Scott, 1979).

Postscript

Years ago, as a young police constable in the Metropolitan Police, I was assisting traffic at a busy junction in St Johns Wood during the morning rush-hour. I was feeling rather elated because the chief superintendent of the division has just passed me in his chauffeur-driven car and with the rear window wound down had called out, 'Well done, Robin; keep up the good work.' I was a new bobby and he recognised me which seemed incredible since I had my back to his car.

Anyway, moments later, as the traffic lights turned green, a car stalled beside me and despite numerous attempts, the driver could not get the engine started again. Cars were now jamming, horns were blaring and I was in the middle of noisy and angry chaos. Impatient and red-faced drivers were shouting at me to clear the blockage. I was not panicking but I was beginning to get desperate as three phases of lights had gone.

Then I saw two workmen in overalls walking on the pavement and, over the noise, I shouted for them to help me push this stranded car out of the junction. They readily came into the road with a few quips like 'A policeman's lot is not a 'nappy one' and ''ow much is the pay?' We got the car moving but had gone only a couple of yards when the man next to me groaned and collapsed to the ground.

His friend and I immediately got down with him; no pulse, no breathing. I yelled at his mate to find a telephone and dial 999 (no mobiles in those days). I did everything I knew to revive him. But his heart had stopped. And so had the traffic in north London.

Later, at the inevitable Inquest, answering questions from the coroner, I outlined what had happened and expressed my deep sorrow to the workman's widow and her family all of whom were sitting in Court. I was devastated of course but his widow came to me after the Hearing.

'I am so sorry that this had to happen to you,' she said. 'I don't blame you in the least. He died helping others. If you need to be, we as a family forgive you completely. Please get on with your life.'

So as you can see, I have experience of being forgiven as well as forgiving. I just want to say that my purpose in sharing with you my thoughts on forgiveness has been an effort to point you to experience a greater quality of life by bearing one another's burdens and binding up each other's wounds. By serving others, we cut across nationalities, religions, human laws, our cultures and personal ambitions. We should be able to talk in positive terms about each other, with a view always to help where necessary. This can escalate from the garden fence, across the street, across the village and town, across the country and across the sea.

The hope we have

We live in a fast-moving age of space exploration, intricate and mind-blowing electronics, new and incredible inventions, huge sophistication in aircraft, ships, motor vehicles, kitchen utensils, far-reaching discoveries in medicine . . . we live in the age of discovery through the brilliance of the mind yet the dreadful parallel is that humanity gets no better. We hear daily reports of shootings, stabbings and other violence; rape and indecent assault, large-scale robberies, pornography and the seedy world of computer images, drug abuse and its accompanying thefts and suicides, alcoholism – on and on and on. We see family love eroded, business corruption (especially in the field of fraud), bombings in the name of religion, and sectarianism. Degradation in our societies locally, nationally and internationally.

It just doesn't balance; for all humanity's progress and for all our brainpower, there is no improvement in behaviour. The spiral is downwards. A universal trait. So where is the hope for our society?

The hope is in Christ.

It *is* possible that we can have that loving, forgiving attitude which is in Jesus. It may, just may, spill over into our school, college, university, workplace and our social and sporting activities. There are many examples in history of people whose gracious way of life has caused heads to turn and lives to change for the better. William Wilberforce, a businessman and politician, was instrumental in having slave-trading outlawed after an almost lifelong struggle. And Captain John Newton, an infamous slave-trader, who was touched by God, sought forgiveness and became a follower of Christ, writing the words of that wonderful hymn, *Amazing Grace*. Look at the lives of Florence Nightingale, the Wesley brothers, and more recently, Mother Teresa. I am sure we could name dozens of others known to us today whose lives because of their Christian faith bring light and hope to others.

In the book of Acts, we read the words of the martyr Stephen, stoned to death by his opponents – 'Lord, do not hold this sin against them' (Acts 7:59). And the words of Jesus on the cross: 'Father, forgive them, for they do not know what they are doing' (Lk. 23:34).

When Jesus was raised from the dead and met with his disciples again, he might have been excused for blaming them all for deserting him – especially his close friend Peter. Jesus was compassionate, however; Peter had persistently denied any knowledge or contact with his Master as we read in Matthew 26:69–75. We know that Peter was fully forgiven and restored by the Lord soon after Jesus' resurrection (see Jn. 21:15–19) and that Peter's renewal was soon evident in the early church as recorded in the book of Acts and in Peter's own writings.

It was Peter who later wrote: 'When they hurled their insults at [Jesus], he did not retaliate; when he suffered, he made no threats. Instead, he entrusted himself to him who judges justly' (1 Pet. 2:23). What a way to live! Does it challenge you as it challenges me?

Perhaps forgiveness really has been the forgotten F word in your experience. How about getting back to basics and getting right with God today? By confessing anything we have not yet had forgiven and allowing his peace to permeate our hearts and lives, we can take on his attitude to face the world. We should be able to walk and talk together even when we don't always agree. We should be able to pray for those in conflict situations especially in the inner cities of the world; we should be praying for our politicians who have to be involved with national and international differences where tolerance needs to be at a premium.

My prayer

Along with the apostle Paul, my prayer is that you, the reader, will be given strength by God's Spirit – 'not a brute strength but a glorious inner strength' as THE MESSAGE puts it – that Christ will live in you as you open your mind and life and invite him in. I pray you will have a resolve and an attitude which means getting right with God and with each other. Forgiveness of others is not the complete answer to life but forgiveness by God is. It may be that we have never regarded ourselves as in need of forgiveness but that is because we have not been honest with ourselves. We know we are not what we ought to be or what we could be and that our objectives in life, while they may be quite honourable, are not the highest. We may feel we *can't* forgive. But is that really so? Are we willing for God to change our hearts? Because he can.

I ask him that with both feet planted firmly on love, you'll be able to take in . . . the extravagant dimensions of Christ's love. Reach out and experience the breadth! Test its length! Plumb the depths! Rise to the heights! Live full lives, full in the fullness of God. God can do anything, you know – far more than you could ever imagine or guess or request in your wildest dreams! He does it not by pushing us around but by working within us, his Spirit deeply and gently within us (Eph. 3:17-20, THE MESSAGE).

That is my prayer for you.

Finally

To complete the circle of this book, I'll finish where I started. Yes, Steve's murder in the course of duty was a very bitter pill to swallow but like all foul-tasting medicines, good has come from it. I have learnt so much about forgiveness and I am sure, therefore, that my heart is the better for it. The truth of Romans 8.28, 'And we know that in all things God works for the good of those who love him' has been real for me. 'If God is for us, who can be against us? . . . Who shall separate us from the love of Christ? Shall trouble or hardship or persecution or famine or nakedness or danger or sword? . . . No, in all these things we are more than conquerors through him who loved us' (Rom. 8:31,35,37).

I thank God for Steve. All the good memories of childhood, the difference that the Lord Jesus made in his life; his great marriage to Lesley and three super kids; his abilities in music, his humour, his expertise as a police officer. I thank God he taught us so much.

May Steve's life and perhaps this book be a real challenge and encouragement to you. And if, by reading it, you find fresh faith to conquer unforgiveness in *your* life, then I thank God.

Prayers

These are the words of Francis of Assisi.

Lord, make me a channel of your peace . . .
That where there is hatred, I may bring love;
That where there is wrong, I may bring a spirit of
    forgiveness;
That where there is discord, I may bring harmony;
That where there is error, I may bring truth;
That where there is doubt, I may bring faith;
That where there is despair, I may bring hope;
That where there are shadows, I may bring light;
That where there is sadness, I may bring joy.
Lord, grant that I may seek rather to comfort than to
    be comforted,
To understand than to be understood,
To love than to be loved.
For it is by self-forgetting that one finds,
It is by forgiving that one is forgiven;
It is by dying that one awakens to Eternal Life.

You might find these words helpful as you think about
forgiving or being forgiven. You have seen in this book,
I hope, that you can be forgiven by God and this

outworking of forgiveness can then flow to others, setting *you* free.

If you have not given your life to the Lord Jesus but you would like to, maybe you can say these words.

> Lord,
> I have seen and understand that you died on the cross for me. You have taken away the punishment for all my wrong-doing, and are willing to forgive me and give me a whole new life on the inside, by your Spirit. Lord, please forgive me for all the times I have wronged you and others. I turn from my sin. Now Lord please fill me with your Holy Spirit and help me start to live for you.
>> Thank you Lord.
>> Amen.

If you have never said this kind of prayer before, you might like to follow it up by looking for local Christians who can help you as you take your first steps in the Christian walk.

It may be that you do know Christ but you are having a very hard time in forgiving someone. This will block your own relationship with Jesus and you will not know the abundance of life he so wants you to have in him, until you let go of your hurts. Remember, you are not letting that person 'off the hook' – God is in control and will work all things out for the good. But you are letting *yourself* off the hook!

> Lord, thank you for dying for *me* on the cross. It is there you took *my* sin so I can be free and know you and have the eternal life you promise. You know how hard it is for me to think about forgiving [name the person or persons] because of what they have done to [me or someone you love]. This is what they have done [tell the Lord in your own words].

Right now [give the date] I choose to roll this burden over to you, knowing that if I forgive, you will forgive me. Give me your power, Lord, to let go of this now. Give me the ability to pray for [name them]. Love them through me, Lord.

>Thank you
>Amen

You may need to pray this prayer more than once as the memory returns. Or you may need to talk it through with a trusted friend or counsellor who can help you when the temptation to pick at old wounds rears its head. It could be that you don't feel ready to pray that prayer at all. You might prefer this one first!

Lord,
Please give me the desire to want to forgive [name the person/persons]. I can't do it, but I believe and trust that you, in me, can do it. Thank you, Lord, for your power is made perfect in weakness.

>Amen

Index